SCHNABEL'S
INTERPRETATION
OF PIANO MUSIC

Photo: Ilse Bing

Artur Schnabel

SCHNABEL'S INTERPRETATION OF PIANO MUSIC

KONRAD WOLFF

FABER MUSIC
in association with
FABER AND FABER
3 Queen Square
London

First published in 1972
As The Teaching of Artur Schnabel
This edition published in 1979
by Faber Music Limited
in association with
Faber and Faber Limited
3 Queen Square London WC1
Printed in the U.S.A.
All rights reserved

ISBN 0 571 10029 5

For
ILSE

Preface

The pianist Artur Schnabel, who studied with Leschetitzky for six years in Vienna and then became one of the major forces in Berlin's musical life for three decades, left Germany in 1933. Many of his pupils, from Sir Clifford Curzon to Leon Fleisher, were originally from Anglo-Saxon countries or, like Schnabel himself, emigrated there. Thanks to this continuum, Schnabel's influence is still vital in England and the United States—whereas we, younger Central Europeans, had to discover this unique musician by ourselves from a geographic, as well as an historic, distance.

I can remember my first, exciting encounter with a Schnabel recording. It was of Beethoven's *Bagatelles,* op. 33, which I heard over Radio Vienna in the early 1950's. The strangely eloquent character of his playing (in one of these *Bagatelles* Beethoven marks "con una certa espressione parlante"), as well as the freedom and courage of a declamation in which the music was steadily animated down to its minutest detail, showed me—who, at that time, approached the pieces which I studied from rather orchestral and vocal viewpoints—a new way of making music. Since then nearly all the Schnabel recordings have been returned to the market and have helped us to become familiar with his playing to the extent to which such a phenomenon can be rendered at all on records, and inasmuch as it is possible to feel truly at home with anything so special and so personal.

The aim of Konrad Wolff's book is to give the reader a better understanding of Schnabel's eminence; at the same time it reaches far beyond Schnabel's personality into the field of general musical problems. I consider it one of the most important books on music

5

in a long time: one of the few which concern and challenge the performing musician directly. It gives a precise insight into Schnabel's method of working, both as a pianist and a pedagogue—and actually not only into his method, but also into his occasional *lack* of method! For in dealing with music he arbitrarily—and most individually—combined whim and reason. To admirers of this great pianist, the book explains several bizarre qualities of his playing while demonstrating, to those interested in music as such, what the problems are which may worry a performer who is capable and willing to reflect upon matters musical. Finally, for the first time in more than a century, we are offered a complete survey of the entire field of interpretation at the piano.

This book does not attempt to represent Schnabel as all-knowing or infallible. Even less does it try to "correct" him: we are thankful to Professor Wolff for having put down his teacher's message so clearly and unpretentiously, and, in contrast to the style of some of Schnabel's own writing, in a presentation of praiseworthy objectivity.

The task of coping with this message must be left to the individual reader. It will be solved more fruitfully the greater the reader's experience, and the stronger his willingness to examine Schnabel's guidelines with a grain of skepticism, instead of misunderstanding them to be dogmatic rules. I myself expect to go on learning from this book, in admiration as well as opposition, for many years to come.

Alfred Brendel

London, 1978

Contents

'I promise nothing complete; because any human thing supposed to be complete, must for that very reason infallibly be faulty.'

Moby Dick, Chapter 31

Preface

Artur Schnabel's pre-eminence as a pianist and his distinguished reputation as a teacher were inseparable. From before the First World War until his death in 1951, he probably taught as many first-rate talents as anyone during that time. Long before he became a resident of the United States he taught many of the outstanding American students, as they were sent by their teachers and advisers to Europe to study under him. After 1930, when the recordings of the Beethoven Society began to appear, coupled with his edition of the Beethoven piano sonatas, the number of his pupils reached well into the hundreds. He loved teaching, and to each pupil he gave his best.

This book is an attempt to pass on to a larger circle of pianists, students, other musicians and lovers of music, the core of his artistic beliefs and his approach to music. The first draft dates back to the time when I myself, beginning in 1936, studied with Schnabel; it was approved, and I was encouraged to enlarge on it. In subsequent years Schnabel reviewed my book in every detail and wanted it eventually to appear as written 'with the collaboration of Artur Schnabel'. After his death in 1951—which made this project impossible—I began to cast the manuscript into its present form, in which the ideas and suggestions are identified as emanations from Schnabel's artistic personality.

In this task I have been helped by pupils and friends of Schnabel's too numerous to list here. I am deeply indebted to all of them. I must mention, however, Mr. and Mrs. Dolf Swing who, acting for the Schnabel Memorial Society then headed by Beveridge Webster, spent many weeks of volunteer work rewriting the first chapters in a more accessible style of presentation: their work became very useful to me when I later revised my manuscript once more.

Theodor Leschetitzky, who taught Schnabel, and his generation saw the task of the piano teacher differently from the teachers of today. The teacher had to prepare the pupil for a virtuoso career. Knowledge of music other than the needed repertoire; improvising; sight-reading; composition, etc., were secondary. Musical problems, as well as technical problems arising out of musical necessities, were rarely discussed. Since then we have discovered that in music many things can be taught which the older generation had to relegate to 'musical instinct'; Schnabel was not the only piano teacher to give his students a musical background, though he was certainly one of the most inspiring and creative. Moreover, he was the only one to convey a general approach covering all possible difficulties to his students, so that, after several years of lessons, they were able to cope with as yet unencountered musical problems that came up in practising. What he said and what he demonstrated by playing during his lessons amounts, in other words, to a complete system. Although several respected and competent pianists, in their or their pupils' collected articles, memoirs, etc., have much to say about a number of musical details, there is no up-to-date book surveying the musical territory of the pianist-interpreter in general. It is indeed astonishing that since the time of Bach's second son, in the 1750s, only one such book, to my knowledge, has appeared: Kullak's *Aesthetik des Klavierspiels* of 1861! The present book, though its conclusions (or at least, some of them) are clearly debatable, certainly comes none too soon to fill this gap.

After the introductory chapters, which deal with the task of the pianist and the basic relationship between music and technique, the main body of the investigation is presented in four sections: (1) articulation of phrases; (2) correct and constructive score-reading; (3) characterization of a composition in performance; and (4) pianistic means and their control. The examples used either stem from actual Schnabel lessons or were given or approved by him during our common work on the first manuscript of this book. They are therefore limited to the music which Schnabel played and mainly taught, which excluded modern masters. Throughout the book, Schnabel's own remarks are indicated as such by quotation marks surrounding them.

I should like to thank my publishers, Faber and Faber, and especially Mr. Donald Mitchell, Mr. John M. Thomson and Mr. Charles Ford for their invaluable help in preparing the manuscript. I am grateful also to Mr. Paul Hamburger for his many constructive suggestions.

For the benefit of American readers, I mention that the British terms 'minim', 'crotchet' and 'quaver' adopted in this book correspond to the American 'half-note', 'quarter-note' and 'eighth-note' respectively.

KONRAD WOLFF

Preface to the Second Edition

A few errors and misprints have been corrected, and some of Schnabel's thoughts more clearly expressed. To this end I received valuable help over the years from many friends, notably Martha Casey, Maria Curcio, Leon Fleisher, Claude Frank, Florence Kirsch, Dika Newlin, Russell Sherman, Erik Tawastjerna, and Tamara Trykar-Lu. I am grateful to all of these, also to Katherine Spielmann for her most valuable help in preparing this edition.

K.W.

CHAPTER ONE

The Task of the Pianist in General

According to Schnabel, the fundamental relationship of an inter-preter to his task rests on his inborn urge towards expression and his feeling for shape. Humility towards the printed score is a foregone conclusion. The performer thus necessarily seeks the ideal of making music which shall be both absolutely faithful and yet completely unfettered. A composition, more than its presentation, ranks supreme in the hierarchy of art, and the performer must be guided only by it. Within those confines, however, he is free, active and formative in a way that is his own special privilege. In a primitive sense, it is he who is the musician, for it is he who produces the sound. He will only be able to perform his task if he makes music quite spontaneously, or as Heine says, if the presentation 'reveals the performer standing on the same free spiritual heights as the com-poser, if it convinces us that he too is free'.[1]

Intense penetration of the letter and spirit of a composition acts as stimulation and leads to its revitalization in performance. The term 're-creation' has often given rise to the misunderstanding that the interpreter can attempt a revival of the personality of the composer at the moment of creation. The futility of such attitudes is generally acknowledged. We know that all interpretive re-creation depends on the awareness of the structure and objective character of a composi-tion.

Schnabel discussed these problems in an absolute and dogmatic way, but behind his utterances was always the intention of leading the young musician to the centre of his task, making it impossible for him to be influenced by extraneous considerations. He frequently

---

[1] *Lutetia*, first report on the musical season of 1843 (March 20, 1843), last paragraph.

emphasized that the interpreter, both when studying and performing, be concerned solely with the music, not with the fact that the art of performing in public is a communication between the composer and the audience. He knew that if the performer became one with the music the audience would feel it, while if he tried to play *to* an audience, he would not be able to do full justice to the music.

Schnabel also warned his pupils against *stylistic generalizations*. He felt strongly that it was unnecessary and sometimes dangerous for the interpreter of music to guide his playing by considerations of the 'style' of a period or the characteristics of a national or regional background. He did not believe that a pianist 'had to have lived in Vienna' in order to play Schubert dances, or in Paris in order to play French impressionists. With his caustic humour he attacked superficial performances of Mozart as 'a masked ball in rococo costume', or warned against Brahms understood as a 'man with the 3 B's of beer, beard, and belly' (*Bier, Bart und Bauch*). This kind of pseudo-stylistic approach he considered irrelevant, and found it distracted from the character of each individual composition. All good composers mean each score to stand on its own, as though there were no other music in existence. Deliberately small tone in Mozart; delayed third beats in Schubert waltzes; unmotivated tempo changes in Schumann; senseless dryness of tone in Bach—all these and other mannerisms were rejected as such by Schnabel. And even in compositions based on folk music such as Hungarian Rhapsodies and Mazurkas, Schnabel assured us that if we concentrated on the individual piece we would find its folklore element. In any case the uniqueness of each work of art, and its quality in belonging to art in general, had to be preserved.

Preconceptions regarding style also restrict the pianist's own understanding of the possible scope of great composers. Not all Mozart's works are 'classical'; not all Bach's are 'baroque'; and it is just where a composer breaks through the stylistic restrictions of his time and nation that the interpreter has to be alert. Often a genius anticipates the style of a period to come. Schnabel explained, played and recorded, the middle section of Brahms's Intermezzo in A minor, op. 116 no. 2, as 'impressionist': his avoidance of phrase separations, his flexibility of tempo, his generous pedalling, and the sonority in which a mood is hinted at rather than expressed–all this is what one would be more inclined to connect with a Debussy piece than with a Brahms intermezzo. Yet Brahms himself would presumably have wished to hear the work in this manner. In the stylistic classification of Brahms as a late romantic or an early neo-classic, however, this interpretation would have no room.

This is not to say that the pianist should not study styles and musical languages. He should especially become extremely familiar with the great works other than piano compositions by the composers whose piano pieces he is studying. It would be very difficult indeed to understand the full meaning of the piano works of Bach, Mozart, Beethoven, and Schubert without a good knowledge of Bach's vocal music, Mozart's operas, Beethoven's quartets, and Schubert's *Lieder*. In a speech for Klemperer[1] Schnabel said 'Creators are not specialists', by which he referred to the various ideas formulated in these paragraphs. By the time a performer is ready to begin the performance, all experiences of other music must be dissolved into the direct experience of the individual piece before him. Schnabel's favourite quotation[2] was Goethe's: 'What is the universal? The single case! What is the particular? Millions of cases!' Each great composition was, to Schnabel, 'all-inclusive, all-embracing', and not comparable to any other great composition, even by the same master. Many older New Yorkers will remember the exaggerated verbal attack he launched on Rudolf Kolisch at a meeting of the American Musicological Society, because Kolisch, with the help of authentic metronome marks, had attempted a classification of tempo 'types' in Beethoven's works. According to him, works of the same 'type' were meant to be performed at the same tempo.[3]

The same caution, finally, is needed in the leaning on *programmatic, descriptive or poetic images* in performing programme and other similarly inspired music. Certain images, of course, are aural rather than visual and cannot be eliminated from the imagination of

---

[1] Reprinted in the *Vossische Zeitung* of 6 December, 1932.

[2] A. Schnabel, *Music and the Line of Most Resistance*, p. 58.

[3] Kolisch's findings were later published in *Musical Quarterly*, 1943, pp. 169 and 291 ff.

the performing musician. 'The humming bird, to which music owes so much, is certainly one of the most legitimate and one of the purest inspirations a performer can have.' Schnabel used this and other images in lessons. He was fond of describing certain types of music as 'processional', such as the middle section of the slow movement of Schubert's posthumous Sonata in B flat major, or the main theme of the slow movement of Beethoven's Sonata in A, op. 2 no. 2. However, he was aware that images like these are limited in scope and are subjective. Music, he said, evokes images, but the reverse is not true: images do not evoke music.[1] His statement was not superfluous, for it happens all too often that in pieces like 'Papillons' programmatic ideas become so fixed in the interpreter's mind that they lead to a distortion of the musical phrase. Good music, even if programmatic and descriptive, is always musically self-sufficient. Exaggerated focusing on programmatic ideas leads to dynamic and rhythmic overstatements, as for instance by an underlining of *echo* nuances. It is true that most of Bach's contemporaries used echo effects as a playful device. But not as an important musical event! The music *continues* in soft repetition, as Schnabel pointed out, and therefore there must be no interruption between the first (loud) and the second (soft) statement of a phrase.[2] He explained this with the help of the beginning of Mozart's A minor Sonata, K.310, bars 16–19 (see Ex. 21).

Theoretical analysis as such is no cure-all either, as Schnabel pointed out. 'It does no harm to know,' he would say. He always encouraged students to find out as much as possible about the structure, harmonies, motivic technique, etc. used in each score. But there is no basis for interpretation in most of this. *Fruitful* analysis

[1] Beethoven, in the programme printed for the première of his *Pastoral* Symphony, inserted a note to the effect that titles are 'rather an expression of feeling than a tone painting'. Nietzsche, perhaps not knowing this, expressed the same thought by stating: 'Even if the tone-poet has spoken in pictures concerning a composition, if for instance he has designated a certain symphony as the *Pastoral*, a passage therein as "The Scene by the Brook", or another as the "Merry Gathering of Peasants", these are likewise only symbolic representations which . . . have no distinctive value of their own as compared to other pictorial expressions.' *Birth of Tragedy* (1870/1), Chapter 6.

[2] But see p. 86.

is the result of spontaneous reaction to some musical detail which puzzles the musician so that he investigates what happens here in particular. To *begin* the study of a new work by analysing its form, in school term-paper fashion, is more harmful than helpful. One example may suffice to illustrate this. An academic outline analysis, as applied to the first movement of Beethoven's Sonata in E major, op. 109, will establish the fact that the first eight bars constitute the first, the ensuing Adagio the second thematic group. If the pianist-interpreter lets himself be guided by this obvious fact, he will make an interruption after the first eight bars to bring out the formal contrast between the different themes and speeds. Nothing could be more wrong. There is one long line that goes from the first note to the end of the exposition, without stop and without a break of any kind. The initial E major chord opens a phrase which is continued until finally the E major key is replaced, in bar 15, by a B major chord implied in the *sforzato* bass on B. Schnabel formulated this as follows: 'The question of form arises here only as one of the *space* to be conquered in one impulse, as inner necessity, as emotion put in motion, as something almost physical.'

During the past century, beginning with Hans v. Bülow, this kind of pseudo-scientific analysis has done much harm. Wherever the facts did not fit the theory they were changed, to the extent of altering actual notes in the score. As opposed to this kind of approach, true analysis is but a clarification and intensification of musical sensitivity, an additional push in the right direction as established by musical instinct. In the opening movement of Schubert's A minor Sonata, op. 42, the initial iambic phrasing, as Schnabel found out, changes during the coda to a trochaic one:

Example 1a, 1b

Analysis can perhaps *explain* why this change occurs, but it could not have *produced* the insight which led to Schnabel's perception. In such cases, musical instinct comes first. It is then confirmed and, in some cases, amended in its findings by analysis. As for the Schubert example, the up-beat phrasing in the beginning is suggested by the three-beat motive which precedes it, whereas in the coda the phrasing must eventually lead into the series of crotchet chords which follows, and this becomes the strongest factor in its presentation.

The task of the interpreter encompasses the right kind of *concentration* during performance (as opposed to that needed for study and practice). On this point, Schnabel was very specific. In high tension—emotional and intellectual—the performer must anticipate the rendering in sound of the entire composition, as a total unit. Schnabel compared this with the intake of a deep breath—deep enough to make the entire performance appear as *one* slow exhalation. If this succeeds, there will be a moment of stillness immediately after the end of the playing; Beethoven, in several of his sonatas—op. 54 in F major for instance—marked this by a *fermata* on the terminal rest (to which Schnabel's edition draws the attention of the reader). In addition, the performer concentrates at every point on the phrase which is coming up and is to follow directly, in order that it may be heard and shaped in the vivid imagination of listening with the so-called inner ear. It is at this point[1] that a *rubato* is planned. Simultaneously, however, the performer also concentrates on what he has just played, checking especially his sonorities. Thus, as Schnabel often emphasized, the performer's inner ear hears everything twice: each little bit is mentally anticipated as well as checked out by later control. If all goes well, these two mental perceptions are blended into one or, as Schnabel phrased it: 'the conception materializes and the materialization redissolves into conception'.

In Schnabel's view, the danger to this complex form of concentration was not so much in being insufficiently as in being wrongly concentrated. Any preoccupation, at the moment of performance (and this is what differentiates performing from certain preliminary phases of practising), with playing right notes, memory, fingerings,

[1] See p. 71 below.

or with thoughts on the 'difficulty' of a section of a piece makes it impossible to concentrate fully in the way here described. This is also where awareness of the various factors discussed in this chapter such as 'thinking of audience reaction', 'style characteristics', 'programmatic ideas', etc., would create a disturbance.

The task of the interpreter, finally, includes his being concretely directed toward the *unity and diversity* within each work he plays. This includes a 'compensation' of surface elements and inner life. The task is carried out in study as well as spontaneously in performance. Schnabel once formulated this idea as follows: 'The performer does not underline anything which the composer has already made obvious. He has to take care of whatever the composer left for him to take care of.' This can apply to almost anything, but it concerns primarily the unity and diversity coexistent in each work. The pianist must stress subtleties of texture underneath an appealing top part tune; but he must hold a top voice tune together when the rhythmic-harmonic structure underneath, as sometimes in Brahms, threatens to destroy the unity of the piece. He will find hidden agitation in an apparently serene composition (as often in Mozart) or inner serenity in an outwardly agitated one (as often in Beethoven). But as he compensates, he must leave the surface as such alone, or else he would disturb the balance which the composer desired.

CHAPTER TWO

Music and Technique

In moments of great intensity, the spiritual and physical aspects of making music can become so completely unified that it is no longer possible to tell where one stops and the other begins. But these two aspects may also sometimes disintegrate to a point where the creative potential of a performer cannot be realized at all. This is mostly due to the fact that music and technique are to a large degree separately trained and developed, and that they undergo partly separate experiences. Their balance and co-ordination therefore remains a principal pedagogical problem. Schnabel was deeply aware of this, and all his teaching showed his effort to bridge this gulf.

The mature performer works for those rare inspirations when his conception of a score becomes one with its physical realization in performance. At such moments technique is more than just the disciplined functioning of the body at the command of the ear: it grows into a physical activity which in turn may stimulate the imagination. Fulfilments of this kind can never be expected, they come unbidden if they come at all, and disappear as suddenly. What we can work for, however, is the elimination of mental-physical gaps by patient and disciplined training of all faculties, mental and physical, *together*. When there are gaps, the physical realization slips away from the mental image. The playing may be musical inasmuch as it is accurate in detail and beautiful in sound, but it lacks the power of communicating the essence of the score. The audience wrongly receives the impression that the performer does not like or does not understand the piece, whereas he is simply unable to bring his conceptions convincingly to the fore. Piano technique, as Schnabel used the term and taught it, is the faculty to establish channels between the sound heard inwardly and its realization in all individualized subtlety, or, as one might say, channels between the 'soul' and 'body' of the interpretation of a score.

The present educational trend makes this goal progressively harder to reach. For while great attention is paid, on the one hand, to scientific analysis and, on the other, to body training, nothing is taught that would enable a student to connect the two. In examinations theoretical knowledge is tested abstractly, and bravura is assessed in piano competitions by what Schnabel called the 'measurable quantities' (speed of octaves and such). Piano technique as such receives much attention, and its level is considerably raised through the elaborate study of its anatomical side and of the pertinent mechanical laws.[1] This in turn causes many teachers to define technique in terms of body relaxation, hand position and the source and quality of physical movement (as in modern dance), all of which has had much beneficial effect, but has also produced some seriously injurious consequences. The use of dumb pianos has become increasingly common, anatomical studies are imposed on students, and gymnastic considerations have led some teachers to building their technical training on just *one* facet of body activity such as spreading elbows, dropping wrists, turning hands in and out depending on the direction of the arm, etc. The more advanced this kind of technical study, the less it helps a pianist with the specific technical problems arising out of the study of individual pieces. A glance at the famous methods of Breithaupt and others confirms this. The authors rarely discuss such technical problems as proportion of sonorities in chord playing, differences between articulated fast scales and glissando-like scales, differences in trill and octave playing between right hand and left hand,[2] etc. This is why Schnabel, on the whole, considered such books more dangerous than helpful.[3]

As a reaction to the over-emphasis on technique, the public, in

[1] O. Ortmann, in *The Physiological Mechanics of Piano Technique* (London, 1929), p. 383, lists seventy-three books and articles on the physiology of piano technique. Hundreds more have since been added.

[2] See pp. 160, 178.

[3] Schnabel, of course, did not live to know the more recent works of Gàt, Neuhaus and others, which might have appealed to him more.

the last fifty years, has been increasingly attracted to intimate performances of piano music by amateurs, conductors and composers. Such music-making, where the personal involvement of each member of the audience often compensates for minor technical imperfections, is at times highly successful. But great music calls for more than loving and loyal performances, and the most magnetic atmosphere cannot replace a reliable interpretive technique.

These were the premises of Schnabel's attitude towards the teaching of technique and constructive practising. Because during lessons he discussed physical problems very little, it has sometimes been assumed that he underestimated technique, especially since in his own public performances his concern for the right articulation and characterization much exceeded his concern for technical security. 'Safety last', he told his students and often praised them when for musical reasons they took technical risks. In reality he was much concerned with technical control gained through practice of specific difficulties in a constructive and imaginative way. Obviously, a general facility of physical movement was needed to practise in the individual ways he demonstrated and to deal successfully with the problems he discussed. In earlier years he provided a general physical training, and he once formulated its principles very clearly in an interview with James Francis Cooke.[1] In this interview the emphasis was on relaxation, especially of the neck and shoulders. In the last conversation I had with him about this book, in the year of his death, he wished me to say here that in all general physical piano training a 'concentration on relaxation' was most essential: 'Tension should be in the forehead only.' He acknowledged the difficulty of this and admitted that he himself had had to struggle for relaxation all through his career, relaxed chord-playing being his special concern.

He never welded his technical ideas into a system, and it would be against his wish for me to do so now. Their realization depends largely on a facility gained by other methods, just as he had gained his through the Leschetitzky training. He saw piano playing as a form of musical speech. 'One speaks upward and forward,' he said,

[1] Printed in *Etude*, February 1922, reprinted February 1952, and included in Dr. James F. Cooke's *Great Men and Famous Musicians* (1925).

'and therefore one must not play downward and backward.' He never used movements in which the arm would be withdrawn from the keyboard in the direction of the body or fall in the direction of the floor. He sat rather low and rather far away from the piano, on a chair with a back, even in concert halls. While the side of his back could swing freely, its central axis remained in place. When his hands, in this body position, touched the keys from close by (Schnabel's hand was hardly ever more than an inch away from the keyboard), a tremendously full and effortless sound went forward and upward from the sounding-board of the piano. In my own words I would perhaps describe this way of playing as one in which the finger stroke is completely *followed through*. The elbow stretches; the upper arm moves forward; the upper part of the finger becomes almost perpendicular. But this is not an independent arm or shoulder action but rather the completion of the motion engendered by the down-stroke of the finger tip. When, especially in a melody, a complete *legato* of successive single notes is required, the follow-through action is slow enough to distribute itself over the several tones of the phrase, which solves the weight-transfer problem very easily.

Schnabel did not impose his way of playing on pupils whose technique, though different, enabled them to have musical and technical control. He looked at his pupils' hands only when something went wrong. The truly taboo types of movements, like 'poking' or 'dangling' fingers, were immediately audible by their unmusical results. The great advantage of his occasional remarks on technique was, of course, that the students could watch him!

In the following chapters I shall try to show in detail how Schnabel successfully connected technical and musical problems in the standard repertoire of his day. In every phrase–literally–he demonstrated these connections to his pupils.

CHAPTER THREE

Articulation—Introduction

'Articulation', as Schnabel used the term quite elastically, refers to the clarification of musical detail by any means available to the performer such as length, loudness, timing, etc. Articulation is a most subtle element in performance, too subtle, most of the time, to be precisely indicated in the score. The rules of articulation which Schnabel evolved were unprecedented. In my opinion they constitute his most original and enduring contribution to the teaching of music. Articulation connects the goal and the means–music and technique. If the student, in a new piece, immediately concentrates on appropriate articulation for each phrase, the technical and musical means are treated simultaneously. His approach to the piece is not merely a mechanical and indistinct rendering of the notes. He does not learn 'first the notes, then the expression'. On the other hand, his effort to be articulate in all respects gives him something concrete with which to work. If a disturbing accent is given on a note that should not be emphasized, the reason may be lack of finger control, of ear discipline or of musical understanding. Technical and musical considerations are so closely tied that in many cases the pianist himself would find it difficult to determine which element causes the fault.

The pianist sometimes imagines he is articulate when he plays all *legato*, *staccato* notes and slurs as marked, observes the time value of each note and rest, and renders the rhythm and dynamics faithfully. But such accuracies do not necessarily amount to essential declamation. Unwritten rules govern subtle nuances of dynamics and rhythm. There are no symbols that would make notation of these subtleties possible, and even if there were, the composer would risk a distortion in the total unity of the work by notating them. Nevertheless the true musician will not miss these nuances if he subjects the score to intense penetration by his eye and inner ear. A sequence of

Example 2

two notes may in reality be a scale which must be heard as such (Beethoven, Violin Sonata in E flat, op. 12 no. 3, Finale). Therefore there cannot be as much emphasis on the grouping by two as in progressions in which the second of the two notes is repeated as the first note of the following group (Beethoven, D minor Sonata, op. 31 no. 2):

Example 3

A rest may terminate a phrase, or it may occur in the middle of it. In the first case, the pianist punctuates, in the second he continues beyond the interruption. The second theme from Mozart's D major Sonata, K.311 (first movement) contains four rests. The first two of these terminate a phrase, the following two occur in the middle of a longer phrase.

Example 4

The above examples concern different aspects of articulation. The Beethoven examples are solved by observing their *melodic* structure, regardless of rhythm. In the Mozart example the long phrase leading to an imperfect cadence on the dominant necessitates an awareness of its *metric shape*, regardless of the melody line. In other cases *harmonic* considerations are paramount. These various aspects will be discussed in the chapters to follow.

Schnabel did not teach articulation systematically. In many cases he would say, 'no accent on A flat' without explaining why, and would not be satisfied until the student could reproduce the phrase without the faintest trace of such an accent. Or he would say, 'play the dominant better (i.e. with more emphasis) than the tonic' (or vice versa); 'bring out the chromatic progression in the middle voices'; 'listen to the dissonance in the ninth chord'; 'pass the third measure', 'play the eighth notes slow and the quarter notes fast', etc. Gradually a pattern would emerge, making these individual comments appear as the logical outcome of a well-balanced system of interpretive values. At times he did explain some of the rules, especially those pertaining to metric divisions and their presentation in performance. We introduce this system here by presenting the rules which concern each musical element separately. But the different elements always combine, and no interpretation is possible unless one is aware of all of them all the time.

When we speak of 'rules' (a term Schnabel did not like) it is for want of a better designation. The rule in this case aims first of all at making the student aware of the problem and secondly at creating good habits for the first approach to a score. Observing the rules intensifies his awareness of musical values, leads to better working habits and occasionally solves technical problems.

Articulation, as discussed here, applies not only to melodies and themes, but equally well to bass lines, inner voices and particularly to so-called 'brilliant passages'. Schnabel expressly denied that any difference should be made between melodies and passages in the sense that the former were to be played more articulately than the latter. He made intensive studies to determine the articulation of every passage (concentrating especially on Mozart concertos) and to prove his point would recall the second subject of the first movement of the A major Concerto, K.488. In the seventh bar a so-called passage (in reality a faster-moving part of the melody) invades a lyrical theme.

Example 5

He also pointed out that *legato* melodies should not be played more articulately than others. The rules of articulation indeed apply equally to *staccato* melodies. An example of a 'singing *staccato*' begins after the initial eight bars of Beethoven's A major Sonata, op. 2 no. 2.[1]

In performing Bach's works, Schnabel was convinced that the exaggerated opposition of short and long, or accented and unaccented notes within a phrase easily obscured the more important aspects of articulation. In general he avoided the accentuation of *single* notes or beats. Articulation was always directly related to the shape of the composition rather than to the single elements of a phrase.

[1] See also the D major episode in the second movement of Beethoven's Sonata, op. 28.

CHAPTER FOUR

Melodic Articulation

The term 'melodic' is here used in its very largest sense. It refers to any upward or downward direction, or fixation of pitch of any part within the musical texture, and not only to what we consciously hear as a so-called melody. In order to observe the natural articulation of melodic lines, it is necessary first of all to perceive the melodic up-and-down *as such*, that is, independently of harmony, rhythm and metre, both in reading and listening.

This is essential in the cases in which a composer preserves the melody while changing the *harmony*, as happens sometimes in sets of variations. In var. 6 of Beethoven's *Eroica* Variations, op. 35, the melody notes of the E flat major theme, unchanged, are harmonized in C minor. Obviously, the presentation of the melody must remain the same as in the theme; in other words its articulation is not dependent on the harmony. To this end the pianist must not let himself be distracted by the left hand. He must listen to the melody as such. Similar examples occur in all *cantus firmus* music, including Bach chorale harmonizations.

Canons and fugues, old and new, offer many examples of *rhythmical* and *metrical* changes in a melodically unchanged sequence (usually the theme itself). Here the essential problem for the pianist is to make the characteristic intervals of the melody, especially the dissonant ones, clearly audible, whatever happens to the rhythm. A case of a different kind is found in the coda of the first movement of Beethoven's last E major Sonata, op. 109: in the most crucial phrase of this section, he purposely uses the same three notes G sharp', C sharp", and B' both for the beginning and for the end, changing them not only harmonically but also in their metrical function within the phrase.

Example 6

Schnabel emphasized the identity of the melodic sequence by making a top-part *crescendo*, *legatissimo*, to C sharp″ in both places. Similarly, he played the end of the first section of Bach's *Italian Concerto* (bars 27–30) so that the double appearance, in the top part, of the sequence F″–E″–F″, despite being in a different rhythm each time, would be perceived in its melodic identity.

Schnabel's teaching of melodic articulation falls into two groups: melodic orientation on one note, and melodic directions.

MELODY LINES ORIENTED ON ONE NOTE

This note may be (1) the point of departure, or (2) the centre of gravity, or (3) the final goal.

(1) The first note of Brahms's Intermezzo in E flat minor, op. 118 no. 6, is to be articulated as the *point of departure* for the unaccompanied melody of twelve notes as a whole. Only three notes are sounded: G flat″ (five times), F″ (four times), and E flat″ (three times), and the melodic line can be described as a long and increasingly futile struggle to hold on to the G flat″ of the beginning. Three times the melody returns to this note from below. Each time there must be a slight emphasis on it. The fourth time, however, it is only passed as an unaccented up-beat in an inverted turn on F″ which resolves downward to the final E flat″ of the melody.

Example 7

p sotto voce

main line

The declamatory nuances indicated here are so small and delicate that they cannot possibly interfere with the unity of the melody.

31

They are not phrasings, only shadings, and Schnabel often said in such instances: 'just for yourself'—meaning that listeners should not be consciously aware of them.

A similar structure is found in the opening of Schubert's Sonata in G, op. 78:

Example 8

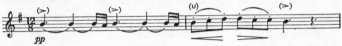

The first B′ is confirmed by a second one, half a bar later. The third B′ however is unaccented (which the pianist must not neglect to watch), being the beginning of a longer phrase leading to the fourth and final B′ in a curve from above.[1]

See also, from Mozart's *Rondo alla turca* (Sonata in A, K.331):

Example 9

Here, after the initial rise, the melody immediately begins to descend in a long sequence of circuitous quavers. The C sharp′′′ at the beginning of the second full measure initiates this descent and must therefore remain unstressed.

When a scale melody ascends and then turns about and descends, the turning point (the top note, that is), in Schnabel's view, already belongs to the descent as its first note and must therefore remain unaccented. Schnabel repeatedly stated, for instance, that beginners should practise ascending C major scales from C only up to B, in order to get into the habit of hearing the top note C not as an end, but as the beginning of the return.[2]

---

[1] The second theme of the Finale of his great C major Symphony is similarly constructed. Schubert here makes his intentions clear by giving accents to all but one (the fifth) of the repeated notes.

[2] This was also recommended by him to overcome the physical problem of playing the fourth finger in the right hand following the fifth. However, the main reason was musical.

(2) Sometimes the principal note forms the *centre* of the melodic line. The melody seems to gravitate around it. Schnabel explained the variation theme from Beethoven's Sonata in E major, op. 109, as circling around E′. This note appears four times: twice it follows the major third above, once the fifth above, and the last time it succeeds the sixth below.

Example 10

Aware of this melodic structure, the pianist will, in the top part, put the weight of the 1st, 3rd, 5th, and 7th bar on their second beats, rather than on their first.[1]

(3) Schnabel paid much attention to the many cases, especially in Schumann, in which the *final note* determines the articulation of a melody. The middle section of no. 4 of *Kreisleriana* consists of two-bar phrases each ending on D′, an octave below where they began. It is not easy to clarify that the melody here, as it were, bites its own tail. Both times, the middle of the phrase is easily heard as an end, where the melody reaches G′.

Example 11a

If the pianist is not careful, the unity of the line will be destroyed by dividing the music into four half-phrases:

[1] This will put more emphasis on these bars than on the other four. Leon Fleisher in a discussion once tried to make out a case for bars 2, 4, 6, and 8, in which either B or B′ is reached either on the second or on the third beat, only finally to agree with Schnabel's analysis: the theme could not remain *molto cantabile*, if the emphasis were thus shifted to the final note of phrases.

Example 11b

The reason is that it is misleading for the ear that the second bar repeats the first exactly at the fourth below. To overcome this distraction, the pianist ought to listen deliberately to the melodic rise from F sharp′ to B flat′ (third to sixth note of example) as a unit.

Schnabel discovered a similar example in the Finale of Schumann's Fantasy, op. 17.

Example 12

Both phrases end on A′. It is important not to stop on the highest note, in the middle of each phrase.

When Schnabel prepared the Finale of Beethoven's *Pathétique* Sonata for his last recital (January 1951), he was intrigued by the B flats which terminate each of the two phrases that form the second subject. In order to make audible what he heard inwardly he separated these two phrases by extending the length of the first B flat′ slightly, and then playing the second quite softly, like an echo of the first:

Example 13

MELODIC DIRECTIONS

These may be upward, downward or stationary (as for instance in pedal points), broken or unbroken. It will be seen in Chapter 10 how melodic direction can become a decisive factor in the structure of compositions. Good taste alone can determine the *extent* to which these directions should be emphasized. The quality of good taste, as Schnabel once stated, is irreducible and must always be trained in addition to all other attributes of a finished artist. But it also partly depends on his personal character, development and age, and sometimes his daily mood as well–and legitimately so–and can therefore not be determined fully once and for all.

Schnabel's approach to melodic directions can perhaps best be exemplified first by his treatment of *pedal points* which, in his terminology, included pitch fixations over changing harmonies in *any* voice, that is, not necessarily in the lowest.

In the Finale of Mozart's Concerto in A major, K.488, the second solo (bars 62 ff.) begins with a pedal point on the note A for four bars, after which the bass goes diatonically up to B and C sharp'.

Example 14

This bass structure increases the momentum as the phrase enters its second half. To make this clear, the pianist must prepare the ground by giving equal emphasis on each of the initial bass tones on A. See also the Handel theme used by Brahms for his Variations, op. 24, especially bar 3, for which Schnabel gave similar instructions.

Pedal points have a melodic substance even when they do not develop into something else, and must therefore be articulate. Schnabel insisted on the articulation of the repeated semiquavers on G' in the C minor variation of Schubert's A minor Sonata, op. 42, second movement, as the principal agent to make this piece come alive; on the articulation and clarity of the final pedal point on low B in the coda of Brahms's B minor Rhapsody, op. 79 no. 1, etc. In the second solo of Mozart's last Piano Concerto in B flat, K.595, Finale, the key-note is maintained throughout the entire phrase.[1] The emphasis due to the pedal point as such must be equally distributed among the four repeated bass notes here, in order to make them sound as regular as chimes. Pianistically speaking, each of these

[1] See Ex. 151.

tones is produced with a separate, individual impulse–which however must not affect the continuity in the upper voices–a dilemma which creates one of the specific technical difficulties arising from musical needs mentioned in Chapter 2, p. 22.[1] In all these instances –to which one must add the 23rd variation of Beethoven's C minor Variations, in which the G below middle C is maintained throughout–the repeated notes should strike the ear with the natural similarity of leaves from the same tree rather than the machine-made similarity of factory assembly-line products. Finally, these pedal points can also occur in the top part, e.g. the insistent F sharp″ in the Trio section of the Minuet from Schubert's G major Sonata, op. 78, and the same F sharp″–possibly written under the influence of Schubert's melody–in the corresponding section of Brahms's Rhapsody in B minor, op. 79 no. 1. Their lively articulation, their chime-like quality which has to be brought out, is one of the main tasks of the pianist as he studies and plays these pieces.

When the melodic direction is *up* or *down*, it is sometimes helpful to try to construct a simplified version of the music in order to determine its long melodic line. In a lesson on Beethoven's Fantasy, op. 77, Schnabel played the first phrase as shown below:

Example 15a

Example 15b

in order to show that the cadence is reached here by descent, and that the melodic line should therefore not be interrupted by over-articulating the rhythmic and melodic detail.

Schnabel was of the opinion that in general, when rise and fall alternate in a melodic sequence, the rise is the more noteworthy event which must be given emphasis. The two directions may be

[1] See also Beethoven, Sonata in D major, op. 10 no. 3, first movement, end of exposition.

combined in a simple pattern, as in the Finale of Mozart's Concerto in C, K.467, bars 128 ff:

Example 16

or in a more elaborate zigzag design, as in the first movement of the same Concerto, bars 270–3:

Example 17

It is of special importance to emphasize melodic rises when they occur in different parts of the bar, as in variation 14 of Beethoven's C minor Variations:

Example 18

The emphasis on rising melody is a characteristic of vocal music. Mozart's slow movements, therefore, both in his sonatas and in his concertos, which are conceived as arias, come to life only when the pianist articulates each rise in pitch so that it stands out, as Schnabel did himself and taught his students to do.

But *how* can it be emphasized? In slow music it is possible—especially in zigzag rises, as at the end of the slow movement of Beethoven's Fourth Piano Concerto

Example 19

to make a slight crescendo from each lower to each upper note.[1] In

[1] I can still hear Schnabel sing 'go up, go up' with each two–note group as he demonstrated this.

places such as Ex. 16 above, a *crescendo* and *diminuendo* as the scales rise and fall, though Kullak and his generation recommended it, would sound horrible to our ears, and Schnabel explicitly warned against it. A much better method here is to put emphasis simply by greater separation of notes in the ascending scales, while playing the descending ones more like a slow *glissando*. In Ex. 17 the best way is to play the ascending five notes as though a second piano· were joined to the first in unison on these notes; that is, without *crescendo*, but slightly fuller than the remaining three notes.

The greatest danger to the clear enunciation of melodic rises is the bad habit many pianists have of accenting the first note of each phrase they play, especially in ascending scales and arpeggios. Most of the time they are not aware they are doing it, because the accent results simply from the habit of dropping the hand on the keyboard as they start. This can be observed in variation 18 of Beethoven's C minor Variations, for instance. Schnabel never tired of repeating that accents have an interrupting effect. Wherever you *want* to create an interruption of phrasing in the midst of an unbroken stream of quick melody notes, you accent the note with which you want the new phrase to begin, especially if they fall between the beats. But wherever you do *not* want to interrupt, your greatest concern must be to avoid accents in places where an interruption could otherwise happen. (See p. 144)

A good example of the complexity of these rules occurs at the end of the introduction to Beethoven's *Emperor* Concerto.

Example 20a, 20b

The tendency here is to accent the first note of each group of four. This not only interrupts the flow of the passage, but also emphasizes the descent of these four notes at the expense of clarifying the gradual rise of the passage as a whole. Schnabel therefore advised his pupils to concentrate on the characteristic intervals linking the last note of each group to the first of the next, as shown in Ex. 20b. This is very simply achieved by separating these two notes sufficiently in performance, without any special accent on either, and without any distorting of phrases.

In some cases, the rise is paradoxically emphasized by a *diminuendo* or by a sudden *piano*, such as Beethoven prescribes for the end of the rondo theme in the Sonata in E minor, op. 90. A *diminuendo* may be used in the slow movement of his Sonata in A major, op. 101, bars 5 and 6. In the first bar of Brahms's Sonata in F minor Schnabel recommended a *diminuendo* from the second to the third beat as the most effective way of clarifying the rise in pitch. The opening theme of the same composer's First Piano Concerto, op. 15, has accents only on the notes of the first, not of the second bar (which is higher in pitch and going up). Where this theme is given to the piano in the recapitulation, Schnabel carefully observed this.

Melodic direction normally begins with the first note and ends with the last. It should not be disturbed, especially not by accents given on top notes, if these occur in the middle. Cf. e.g. bars 16 and 18 of the first movement of Mozart's Sonata in A minor, K.310:

Example 21

Here no accent should be given on C'''.

At times the unity of a long melody can be supported by unobtrusively strengthening certain melodic rises which occur in the middle, especially those *from* a down-beat *to* a weak beat (e.g., the second theme of Schubert's B major Sonata):

Example 22

and those happening over dissonant intervals. The latter is quite frequent in Bach's themes, but also occurs in Beethoven, for instance in the opening movement of the *Waldstein* Sonata, bars 31–33:

Example 23

and at the corresponding place in the *Archduke* Trio, bars 49–51:

Example 24

Schnabel was extremely sensitive (perhaps even oversensitive) to disturbing melodic accents in the middle of a phrase, and he therefore also ruled out the customary underlining of *appoggiatura* notes in lyrical themes, as in the opening bar of the slow movement of Beethoven's Sonata in C minor, op. 10 no. 1:

Example 25

Double care is recommended when the top note occurs on a down-beat, as in the second theme of the Beethoven Sonatina in G major, op. 49 no. 2:

Example 26a   Example 26b

Example 26c

The top note must be heard as an *appoggiatura* (26b), and Schnabel's recording of this phrase, all three times it occurs, suggests that, in order to get away from the down-beat fixation, he heard it in a (hidden) $\frac{3}{4}$ metre (26c).

Nobody played Brahms's Second Piano Concerto for Schnabel

without being told that the E flat''' on the fourth beat of the first solo bar must not have an accent.[1]

As I have already described, in scale-like passages Schnabel sometimes avoided top note accents by thinking of the top note as the unaccented beginning of the descent rather than the end of the ascent. Sometimes (also for technical reasons) he phrased toward the note *following* the top note, as in the example (p. 99) from Mozart's Piano Concerto in A, K.488, in which he directed his playing to the eleventh semiquaver (the second high D''') in the first bar, and correspondingly to high B'' in the following bar.[2]

Finally, when within a lyrical melody the same note is played three times in succession, the first and third being *on* the beat, ·Schnabel liked to emphasize the one in the middle, apparently to counteract the tendency to give even the slightest metrical accent. In the Finale of Beethoven's Sonatina in G, op. 49 no. 2, his edition suggests:

Example 27

(————————) (*f*) [Schnabel Edition markings]

and in the final Rondo of Schubert's posthumous Sonata in A, he played the second subject with this articulation:

Example 28

(———<———>———)

---

[1] See p. 148 and Ex. 176. [2] See Chapter 12, Ex. 112.

CHAPTER FIVE

Harmonic Articulation

The aim of harmonic articulation is, very simply, to clarify the successive harmonies, their functions and their colours, as though one were playing a continuo part. Unlike melodic articulation, this involves, of course, all the parts of the musical texture. In order to be able to do this the performer must obviously have learned to hear harmonies as such, without regard to melody and rhythm. To this effect it is useful to study classical variation sets, because must harmonies and harmonic rhythms remain whereas the melodic and rhythmic patterns change from variation to variation. In the slow movement of Mozart's Piano Concerto in B flat major, K.450, bar 10, Schnabel recommended making a *crescendo* from the harmony of the first beat (C minor) to that of the second (A flat major); and this had to be repeated in every variation (bars 34, 42, etc.).[1]

A sudden change in the melody or in the rhythm sometimes makes the performer forget that the harmonic progressions continue nevertheless: to understand the last seven bars of the opening movement of Beethoven's Sonata in A flat, op. 110, it is advisable to play just the principal notes once:

Example 29

Despite the sudden change in motion and register which occurs between the first two bars in this example, they belong harmonically

[1] See Ex. 182.

together as the opening bars of a harmonic cadence, and this is why Schnabel in his edition–to the bewilderment of many readers–groups them within the same metrical period.

Harmonic changes do not necessarily accompany the end of a phrase. If the harmony continues into the new phrase the performer must enter it, as it were, on tip-toe. For instance, many classical sonata subjects are formed so that in the first four bars, tonic (T) and dominant (D) alternate in sonnet fashion: T–D–D–T whereas the melody is symmetrical as bars 3 and 4 rhyme with bars 1 and 2. This structure occurs, for example, at the beginning of Beethoven's Sonata in C, op. 2 no. 3. The harmony of the second bar is a pure dominant, to which the third bar adds the dominant-seventh. Yet according to Schnabel's explicit teaching, this bar must be heard as continuation of the second, and should therefore be without accent in the bass, so that the harmonic near-identity of bars 2 and 3 becomes audible. As a result the two C major chords at the beginning and end of the phrase are emphasized, and this compensates for the (otherwise trivial-sounding) symmetry of the right-hand melody:

Example 30

From the performer's–not the listener's–viewpoint the intensity of a harmony increases in inverse proportion to its duration: the shorter the latter, the more it wants emphasizing. The first four bars of Schubert's *Moment Musical* in F minor, op. 94 no. 5, consist of three bars of tonic against one bar (the 3rd) of subdominant:

Example 31

This bar has to be accented so that the last two bars emerge as a plagal cadence. A similar example is found in the bridge passage of Beethoven's Sonata in D major, op. 10 no. 3, first movement.[1] Here it is the inverted dominant-seventh chord in the second half of the first bar that is easily drowned in the surrounding sea of tonic (B minor) harmonies.

The texture provided by the composer also influences harmonic articulation. On rare occasions Schnabel made a passage sound new and different by emphasizing a thin chord that the composer had neglected. In the very opening of Chopin's Sonata in B minor, for instance, the subdominant harmonies on the third and fourth beat of the first bar are considerably fuller than the tonic chord which precedes them. Schnabel, to establish an equality which he felt was needed, made a slight *sforzato* accent in the left hand on the second beat, which gave the bar a syncopated character. Moreover, he played the second beat quite early so that it completed and re-emphasized the preceding down-beat, the pedal being held throughout the first two beats. The following subdominant he played relatively softly, as an upbeat to bar 2:

Example 32

In order to articulate a harmony one must first determine which harmony was in the composer's mind. This is not always easy in the case of unison textures, etc. In Chapter 8 we are going to encounter a few doubtful cases of this sort. Schnabel was fond of mentally harmonizing the unaccompanied chromatic scales which he found in the scores of the classical masters—either as augmented triads (each fourth note being a harmony note) or as diminished-sevenths (each third note being a harmony note); the latter, for instance, in the coda of the finale of Beethoven's Sonata in D minor, op. 31 no. 2:

[1] See Ex. 67.

Example 33a

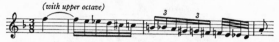

Example 33b

In classical music, unusual chords and startling dissonances are often concealed from the superficial listener by being prepared, as some notes are held over from before, or simply by being played at great speed. An example for the former occurs in bars 34 and 38 of the Allegro of the opening movement of Beethoven's *Les Adieux*, op. 81a:

Example 34

The sharp dissonance between D''' in the right hand and C sharp' in the left is not usually heard, because the pianist, by the time he plays the C sharp', has already forgotten the D''', and also because he plays more E' than C sharp' in the left hand.

As an illustration of how harmonic finesse can get lost simply through fast speed, and of how carefully Schnabel always listened to the music he played, it is worth reporting that he once asked his students, as a quiz, to identify the composer of the following sequences:

Example 35a

He certainly surprised us when he gave the answer: Mozart! This dissonant sequence–which sounds deceptively simple when played in time–stems from the coda of the Finale of the Sonata in B flat, K.333:

45

Example 35b

It is also part of the harmonic aspect of articulation to give pecu-
liarities in part-writing their due, such as deliberate or conspicuous
parallel fifths. I remember two examples of this which Schnabel
pointed out in lessons: Schubert's posthumous Sonata in C minor,
Finale, bar 249:

Example 36

and Mozart's last Sonata in D major, K.576, Finale, bar 105:

Example 37

But wherever the composer did *not* intend to point to the parallel
fifths they should be dissimulated by ways of phrasing. When, in
bar 21 of the Adagio of the *Pathétique*, Beethoven allows $^{G'}_{C'}$ in the
bass to be followed by $^{E\ flat'}_{A\ flat'}$, he wants these two chords to sound as
if they were being played by different instruments. In performance
Schnabel separated them by a complete *caesura*.

Schnabel for the most part rejected the old rule[1] that dissonances
have to be played more loudly than their consonant resolutions.[2] His

[1] C. P .E. Bach, *Versuch über die wahre Art das Klavier zu spielen*, I, section 3,
no. 29.

[2] But soft and quick dissonances must be played and listened to distinctly,
especially when they are immediately resolved. E.g. the ninths between the two
parts in Beethoven's Sonata in A flat, op. 110, first movement, bars 22 f. The idea

rule was more specific and subtle: in a dissonant chord which is supposed to sound harsh, the notes which contain the sharply dissonant interval–such as a major seventh–must be played louder than the others. In a dominant-(minor) ninth chord the clash occurs between the root and its ninth. These two notes, no matter where they are located within the full chord, must be louder than the three remaining ones. Usually players do emphasize the ninth, but more often than not they ignore the equally important root note. As a practice device, in such cases, Schnabel suggested playing just these two notes–root and ninth–alone at first, repeatedly, to let their harsh sound sink in so that the pianist could still hear it clearly in the full chord when all the notes were played.

C. P. E. Bach's rule failed, in Schnabel's opinion, because it mis-judged the true relationship of dissonance and resolution. They are equally important. If a dissonance that occurs *on* the beat is resolved *after* the beat, the dissonance does not need any help from the per-former, but the resolution does. Schnabel occasionally went almost overboard 'taking care' of it. In Mozart's Sonata in G major, first movement, bar 33, he marked these *crescendo* signs in the copy belonging to a pupil:

Example 38

I doubt, however, that he would himself have played the passage quite like that in a performance. But he certainly considered these *crescendi* a lesser evil compared to dropping the notes which contain the harmonic resolution. A similar example is found in the Trio of the Scherzo of Beethoven's Sonata in D, op. 10 no. 3:

Example 39

behind this rule was first formulated by Schoenberg, *Harmonielehre*, third edition, 1922, pp. 389 ff.

The numerous endings in Polonaises in which a dominant-seventh chord is resolved on the third and last beat also belong to this category. And here are three more examples at random, from Beethoven's Bagatelle, op. 126 no. 5; from his Sonata in E, op. 109, third movement, variation 4; and from Schumann's *Carnaval* ('Arlequin' bars 7–8):

Example 40

Example 41

Example 42

Special events in music call for special handling by the performer. Beethoven was fond of scales in complete sixth-chords. We find them as early as the Trio of the Minuet of his first Sonata in F minor, op. 2 no. 1, and as late as the Finale of the Sonata in A, op. 101, at the beginning of the recapitulation. For the purposes of this book, Schnabel gave me the following example from the first movement of Beethoven's Fourth Piano Concerto:

Example 43

He explained that the difference between these passages and simple scales in sixths is harmonic: a scale in *sixths* is heard as one harmony,

48

whereas, when the sixth-*chords* are played with sufficient clarity of the extra note (the one in the middle), they each carry enough of their own harmony to suggest quick harmonic changes from chord to chord. The rule for the performer, as established by Schnabel, is therefore to emphasize the middle notes, all of them—that is, the thirds above the bass, or, as one could also define them, the fifths above the root. In Ex. 43 it means, practically speaking, as Leon Fleisher once formulated it: 'play the left thumb clearly'.

The most important problems of harmonic articulation arise in connection with *harmonic cadences*. As with melodies, harmonic progressions within the same phrase have a direction towards the end concretely realized in the final cadence. The task therefore, generally speaking, is to lead the listener to the final chord as definitely as possible. When the cadence is an authentic one, this means that the dominant (or dominant-seventh) chord which is next to last, and which usually follows a second inversion (six-four) chord of the tonic chord, must be played lightly. Or as Schnabel always called out to his students: 'Pass the dominant!' The first eight bars of the initial theme of Beethoven's Sonata in E flat, op. 31 no. 3, are, harmonically speaking, a cadence: subdominant (with added sixth) for three bars; six-four chord of the tonic reached chromatically via a diminished-seventh chord, for the next three bars, and dominant-seventh leading to final tonic chord in root position, in the last two. Beethoven's performance markings make this example interesting:

Example 44

The six-four chord is reached *crescendo* and *ritardando*; it is then held in a *fermata*, after which the next bar—dominant-seventh—is light and quick. All this, though it is more emphatically enunciated than we would expect in an ordinary cadence, basically corresponds to the normal routine which Schnabel expected any pianist to follow in any such cadencing harmonic sequence.[1] In order to play bar 7 lightly, the essential requirement is that there should be no emphasis on the down-beat in the left hand. Similar examples: Beethoven, Sonata in F minor, op. 2 no. 1, third movement, end of first section:

Example 45

Mozart, Concerto in C, K.467, Finale, bars 151 ff.:

Example 46a

Example 46b

Schubert, Impromptu in C minor, op. 90 no. 1, bar 77:

Example 47

[1] Only the continued *piano* marking for the last measure of the example (though it is of course justified by the immediately following change of register and repeat of the same phrase in high treble) deviates from the normal course of events, as Schnabel pointed out. Normally there could be a slight *crescendo* from bar 7 to bar 8 in such cadences or, conversely, a drop in sonority.

Obviously, though, there have to be exceptions wherever the individual character of the composition requires or permits them. In the Scherzo of Schubert's posthumous Sonata in B flat, Schnabel said of the first eight bars: 'Play measures 4 and 7 best' (= heaviest).[1] His recommendation was probably based on his intuitive awareness of the harmonies: instead of the usual root position, bars 6 and 7 present the sub-dominant and dominant-seventh chords, each in the second inversion. This favours the bass note C' in bar 7, as it comes from and goes back to B flat.

In plagal cadences, the subdominant which precedes the final tonic is always emphasized so that the end is reached *diminuendo*, corresponding to the declamation of the word 'Amen'. See the very end of Chopin's B minor Scherzo; Mozart's Concerto in A, K.488, first movement, bar 4 of the solo opening (*diminuendo* from the second to third beat).

Whatever one may decide in each individual case, one can never stress *both* dominant and tonic, just as in a verse reading one cannot stress *both* verb and subject. In bar 8 of Weber's *Invitation to the Dance*, you can accent either the up-beat or the ensuing down-beat, but not both. Therefore, either:

Example 48a

or:

Example 48b

but not:

Example 48c

While in a cadence the dissonance (dominant-seventh) *precedes* the tonic, this is not necessarily so earlier in a phrase: here the tonic

[1] See Ex. 70.

chord may *lead into* the dominant-seventh. In the second thematic group of the opening movement of the *Hammerklavier* Sonata,

Example 49a

Schnabel was sometimes inclined to hear and therefore phrase the music as sketched below in its principal notes:

Example 49b

A similar structure, similarly played by Schnabel, is the Sonata in C, op. 2 no. 3, Finale, bars 30 ff: the two *sf.* notes are up-beats to the next bar. In the final rondo of Schubert's Sonata in G, op. 78, bars 35–37, Schnabel, who played this movement quite fast, felt that each phrase extended to the third beat of the bar, ending on an altered chord:

Example 50

The dissonances are resolved each time only when the next phrase begins, and Schnabel added to the piquancy of this harmonization by waiting after each such phrase for the fraction of a second in a caesura, but without disturbing the pulse or the tempo. In both the Beethoven and the Schubert example this interpretation is based on the score inasmuch as there are accents marked by the composers which, if strictly observed, will interrupt the music at precisely the places which Schnabel was apt to treat as phrase endings, as here

52

described. It must be added, however, that he was not entirely consistent, and would change the phrase groupings occasionally.

In so-called imperfect cadences, finally, that is, cadences at the end of the first half of a melody which lead into the dominant from where the second half then takes its departure, the supertonic is usually emphasized as it precedes the (half-)closing dominant chord. Mozart liked to repeat imperfect cadences several times, and Schnabel worked out a more subtle articulation for these. Here are two, similar, examples, one from the Finale of his Sonata in B flat, K.570

Example 51

and the other from that of his last Concerto, in the same key, K.595.

Example 52

In both examples Schnabel would play the supertonic-seventh 'better' the first two times, it being the newer, more eventful one of the two chords; but the third time he would 'pass' it in order to reach the closing dominant chord with more decisiveness. Speaking in practical terms, no accent would be permitted in the left hand as the pattern starts to repeat for the last time.

Modulations do not lend themselves to fixed rules of articulation. Obviously, in changing to a nearly-related key, the *new* notes have to be clearly enunciated (e.g. the F sharp when going from C major to G major) as they are played for the first time. Modulations to a remote key, on the contrary, often require an emphasis on the (perhaps remaining) shared note; and this is particularly true of enharmonic changes. In Schumann's 'Papillons', no. 9, for example, Schnabel insisted on a very clear rendering of the final A sharp' (left thumb) since it changes into B flat at the very beginning of the next piece.

Even *single notes* can have a harmonic importance which ought to prompt the interpreter to follow them consistently, especially when they have a function as leading notes, such as the B, two and a half bars before the final Prestissimo in Beethoven's *Waldstein* Sonata, op. 53, which must be heard more distinctly than the D' and F' sounded simultaneously.

Finally, it is important to remember that in music with atonal implications the articulation consists of *not* suggesting harmonic progressions which the composer did not intend. This can also happen in classical music. Schnabel understood the opening of the second half of the final variation in Beethoven's Sonata in E, op. 109, thus:

Example 53

He conceived the *staccato* notes, which come here at the opening of each group of four, as non-harmonic notes, producing at times a highly dissonant sound, in accordance with the character and development of this variation, of which this is one of the crucial moments.

Harmonic and metric articulations are interdependent, because harmonic and metric tensions usually come and go together. The next chapter is therefore a necessary complement to this one.

CHAPTER SIX

Metric Articulation

Rhythm and metre can be thought of as separate categories in the element of time. According to classical definitions (Riemann) metre relates to heavy-and-light, rhythm to long-and-short. For purposes of clarification let us say that metre provides the frame, rhythm the picture. The pattern ♫ ♩ in the main theme of the third movement of Brahms's Third Symphony is such a 'picture'. Brahms places this rhythmic pattern in different ways within the 'frame' of a ⅜ metre. At its first appearance it begins on the up-beat and ends on the down-beat.

Example 54

In the following bar it begins on the down-beat and ends on the second beat.

This structure creates two problems of performance, one rhythmic and one metric. Rhythmically, it must be made clear that the pattern is identical both times. But the metric articulation must make the listener aware of the up-beat rhythm as the pattern begins, and of the feminine ending, as it is repeated. This obviously endangers the rhythmic articulation, which aims at the identity of the two appearances of the pattern. This example shows that a natural antinomy exists between metric and rhythmic articulation, which has to be solved individually in each case.

As I am dealing first with metric articulation, let us look first at single bars and then at metrical periods.

THE SINGLE BAR

In every metre ($\frac{4}{4}$, $\frac{3}{4}$, $\frac{6}{8}$, etc.) the down-beat has a natural weight in excess of the other beats. In the teaching of the later nineteenth century (based on eighteenth-century theory), the down-beat therefore received a metrical accent. In elementary piano teaching this rule is observed to this day. To break it was one of Schnabel's most emphatic goals. He was convinced that in tonal music the composition itself quite distinctly establishes the down-beat and the metre in the great majority of cases—why then underline the obvious? Its over-emphasis necessarily obscures all the other beats, and more important, interferes with the melodic direction whenever it extends beyond one bar. This happens especially in passage work, but also in melodies, as in the first movement of Mozart's Concerto in G, K.453:

Example 55

Whenever a metric accent on the down-beat is imperative it is meant as an emphasis of the lowest tone (in accompanied music) rather than as a melodic accent. A stress on the down-beat is not necessarily made by playing it loudly, but often by phrasing towards the down-beat or by lingering on the first note (or chord) of the bar for a fraction of a second.

An emphasis on the down-beat was ordered by Schnabel only when the down-beat was followed by a syncopated rhythm, as in the second subject of the first movement of Beethoven's Sonata in G, op. 31 no. 1.

The standard rule which proclaims that syncopated notes be accented must be applied with great flexibility. Schnabel spent much time dealing with each case individually. First of all, syncopation accents are not of the same nature as ordinary accents. They must resemble up-bows on a stringed instrument. Schnabel requested them to be played in a '*quasi-vibrato*' so that they would appear pushed up rather than weighed down. He recommended listening to the following down-beat (on which no note is struck) 'as an echo' of the syncopation,[1] as in bars 45 ff. of Schubert's *Wanderer* Fantasy and the repeated G major chords preceding the inversion of the fugue in Beethoven's Sonata, op. 110.

Secondly, wherever there is a succession of syncopated notes, the syncopation accents must be differentiated. When, for instance, in $\frac{2}{4}$ the accompaniment consists of syncopated quavers the second and fourth quavers should not be equally loud. In fast tempo, syncopations are heard after-the-beat rather than anticipating the beat, and therefore the earlier note is the louder note. There are many such examples in Schubert's works, for instance bar 126 of the Impromptu in C minor, op. 90 no. 1.[2]

Example 56

Schubert often implies syncopations where they are not clearly indicated. Schnabel understood the accompaniment for the *Moment Musical* in F minor, op. 94 no. 3 to read as follows:

Example 57

He thus played the first top F in the left hand louder than the second and gave a discreet down-beat emphasis to the first quaver of each bar.

---

[1] See the Scherzo of Beethoven's Cello Sonata in A and Czerny's explanations on the execution of Beethoven's fingerings. (*Über den richtigen Vortrag der sämtlichen Beethovenschen Klavierwerke*, ed. P. Badura-Skoda, reprinted Vienna, 1963, p. 90.)

[2] See also the second subject of the Finale of his Sonata in B flat.

The problems involving metric articulation can be further complicated by difference in metres, between $\frac{2}{4}$, $\frac{3}{4}$, $\frac{4}{4}$, etc. In common time the principal metric problem comes in dealing with the third beat. Many musicians either ignore it altogether or emphasize it equally with the first beat. The truth always lies somewhere between these extremes. What is true of the whole bar is also true of the half bar. In this way the articulation of Alberti basses is partially solved. Schnabel was very much concerned with playing these beautifully rather than mechanically and considered the beginning of Mozart's Sonata in C, K.545 and the slow movement of Beethoven's *Spring* Sonata in F, op. 24 to be particularly difficult. In such places the performer's attention must be directed towards doing enough–but never too much–with the third note in each group of four.

In a $\frac{3}{4}$ metre, theoretically speaking, the natural weight of the second beat is greater than that of the third. We hear the second beat as a continuation of the down-beat, as in a trochaic mode. Therefore, if we think only in terms of metre, ignoring melodic and harmonic configurations, the three beats are actually only two: $\overset{\text{heavy,}}{1\,2}\ \overset{\text{light}}{3}$. When the left hand in a $\frac{3}{4}$ metre plays only a second beat and not a third, as in both sections of Schubert's Impromptu in E flat, op. 90 no. 2, the second beat accents marked by the composer must therefore be played as syncopation accents. In the absence of a third beat the second beat loses its connection with the down-beat and fulfils the function of the third beat, as in a syncopation.[1]

Complex metres such as $\frac{5}{4}$ and $\frac{7}{4}$ are usually articulated as a combination of $3+2$ or $4+3$, etc. 'The authentic $\frac{5}{4}$ measure, however, is $2+1+2$.'

METRIC PERIODS

Much more subtle and complex than the articulation of single bars are the problems which arise in dealing with metric periods. More than most musicians, Schnabel devoted great attention to these problems and arrived at a number of conclusions for the performer.

Metric periods and single bars have a general resemblance not unlike that between stanzas and lines in poetry. Both have a given length and both are composed of alternating heavy and light beats.

[1] See also p. 136.

But there the resemblance stops. Whereas the time signature informs us of the number of beats in each bar and the position of the heaviest beat (the down-beat) we have no general information concerning the metric period. The normal length of a metric period is sometimes considered to be four or eight bars. The truth is, however, that the length of each period varies considerably even within one section of a composition. Each period must be identified individually by the careful study of melodic phrases, harmonic cadences, repeated rhythmic patterns, etc. Schnabel took great pains to establish the length of every period and considered this analysis crucial in cases that were at all questionable, although he was aware that the results always remain somewhat uncertain. In his editions of Beethoven's and Brahms's works he indicated the first and last bars of irregular phrases by roman numerals. He marked his own music in the same way and, as his fingerings were memorized and not pencilled in, the metric numerals are the only marks to be found in the scores he owned. 'As I start a new metrical period,' he explained, 'I must know in advance how long I have to play, whether for six or eight or twelve bars.'

Finding the length of each period is, however, only a preliminary task. The performer must then divide each period into what Schnabel called light and heavy bars. Each period requires an individual decision. A 'normal' half-period of four bars includes four first beats or four down-beats. But these four down-beats are not equally heavy. Whereas, in a single bar, the heaviest point is at the beginning, in a metrical period it usually falls at the end.

Any attempt to discover the proper articulation of metric periods naturally involves the idea of symmetry, with all of its aesthetic implications. While in very simple music (nursery rhymes, etc.) the third and fourth bars often correspond exactly to the first and second in a Light-Heavy-Light-Heavy order, the music of the classical epoch displays a strong desire to get away from this symmetry wherever possible. The second half of the thematic subject in a classical sonata almost always deliberately departs from the metrical structure of the first. The thematic material used by Haydn, Mozart and Beethoven is very often no different from that used by lesser composers of the time, but as the material is developed throughout the phrase it acquires its individual shape.[1] As Schnabel said in jest, 'The genius of a composer begins with the fifth bar.' This knowledge is essential for the performer inasmuch as it leads him to counteract symmetry by stressing the asymmetrical characteristics of the phrase. This sustains the long line of the composition where, melodically speaking, the second half of a metric phrase or half-phrase merely rhymes with the first. In these cases Schnabel advocated groupings of H-L-L-H or H-H-L-H or occasionally L-H-H-L.[2] The following are some illustrations from Schnabel's teaching.

Certain types of basic four-measure themes in Beethoven sonatas seem to invite the performer to a symmetrical articulation of L-H-L-H. I refer again[3] to the first four bars of the Sonata in C, op. 2 no. 3 as well as the second theme of the first movement of the *Waldstein* Sonata, op. 53. The melodic pattern of the second half duplicates that of the first. The two halves however are not harmonically symmetrical. The case of op. 2 no. 3 was analysed above, cf. Ex. 30. Schnabel here recommended H-L-L-H, emphasizing the tonic harmony as both the beginning (positively establishing the key) and the goal of the phrase. The dominant harmony does not need any emphasis since it occurs in two successive bars. For the performer this means that he must start with a slight metric accent, make a *diminuendo* to the down-beat of bar 2, and remain soft throughout bar 3, so that the last down-beat sounds like reaching a goal pursued from the beginning. It may be, though, that the performer wishes to clarify the harmonic progressions. In that case the second bar should be heavier than the first, and the third heavier than the last: this would underline the tonic-dominant progression in the first half, and the dissonance in the beginning of the second. This L-H-H-L order would perhaps sound artificial, but at least it, too, would break the symmetry and thus counteract what the German writer on music August Halm[4] considered to be the 'trivial' element in the thematic structure of the Viennese masters.

[1] See the author's article on J. S. Schroeter in *The Musical Quarterly*, 1958, p. 359, ex. 13.

[2] H = heavy, L = light.

[3] See Chapter 5, Harmonic Articulation, p. 43.

[4] *Von Zwei Kulturen der Musik*, Munich 1920, p. 190.

The harmonic progressions in the example from the *Waldstein* Sonata

Example 58

are more involved. The first bar contains three different harmonies of which Schnabel considered the last, the chord of the relative minor, 'most important'. There are two different harmonies in the second bar, the first of the two bass notes leading to the second. In contrast, the fourth bar at once establishes the dominant note B for the entire bar. Moreover, the end of bar 2 (subdominant) leads into bar 3 (second inversion of dominant-seventh). Here Schnabel taught the order H–L–L–H, as in the example from Beethoven's op. 2 no. 3, if for different reasons: it rules out any *crescendo* in bar 2 and effectively offsets the melodic symmetry.[1]

The same order is almost endemic in Schubert's themes, e.g. the second episode in the final rondo of his Sonata in G, op. 78:

Example 59

---

[1] Some of Beethoven's symphonic opening themes make an interesting study. In the first four bars of the Pastoral Symphony the harmonies are T–D–T–D (the last three notes being identical in each half), and in those of the Eighth Symphony they are T–T–D–D. Various possible metrical orders come to mind here.

as well as the minuet theme:

Example 60

The first example shows how melodic and metric articulation can be different yet compatible: Schubert's *melody* accents fall on light bars. In the second example – in which the accents in the score correspond to the metric order – the pianist must not be misled by the apparent doubling of the bass in bar 3: the two F sharps belong to different parts! A similar articulation can be heard in Schnabel's recording of the Finale of Schubert's Trout Quintet. The four bars of each phrase of the theme are sub-divided in the same manner.

Example 61

There are some instances where the melodic structure of the first half of an eight-bar period necessitates an articulation of H-H-L-H. In such cases bar 1 offers the first presentation of the melody in a movement which lunges forward, bar 2 the second presentation, after which the theme, strengthened in its energy, moves beyond bar 3 in one line to the end of the phrase in bar 4. See, for example, the second movement of Beethoven's Sonata in E, op. 109,

Example 62

the Finale of Mozart's Concerto in B flat, K.456,

Example 63

the Trio of Schubert's *Moment Musical*, op. 94, no. 6,

Example 64

and Mozart's *Rondo alla Turca*, K.331, Finale.

Example 65

These are places where Schnabel would instruct his pupils to 'pass the third bar'. Concerning the Beethoven example, he pointed out that almost the entire main section consists of continual four-bar phrases in a structure of H-H-L-H. 'Passing the third bar' usually includes avoiding accents in the top part as well as in the accompaniment (in the Mozart examples for instance), and any pupil could expect to hear Schnabel exclaim 'No accent!' if any stress remained on the down-beat of bar 3.

Occasionally one finds other combinations of heavy and light. The beginning of the Minuet in Schubert's posthumous Sonata in C minor implies a L-H-H-L articulation.

Example 66

However, the length of the entire theme is metrically irregular and bar 4 could be understood as being the first bar of the next phrase.[1] A H-H-L-L articulation was understood by Schnabel in the 'bridge passage' theme from Beethoven's Sonata in D, op. 10 no. 3:

Example 67

The symmetrical or 'normal' articulation of L-H-L-H appears when there is no danger of too much symmetry, and especially when the first bar has an up-beat character, as for example at the beginning of Beethoven's Sonata in A flat, op. 110. The rondo theme from Mozart's Concerto in A, K.488 has L-H-L-L.

Once the structure of a four-bar period is recognized it is usually not difficult to combine two four-bar periods in the larger unit of an eight-bar period. As Schenker stated, in most cases the first half ascends melodically, the second descends. Since the descent almost always resolves into the expected and normal cadence, it is often necessary to give more weight to the end of the first half, the imperfect cadence. For example, in the rondo theme of Mozart's Concerto in C, K.467, a metrical *poco crescendo* is needed between bars 3 and 4 but not between the last two bars.

Example 68

Cf. also the theme of Brahms's *Handel* Variations:

Example 69

Cf. also the Scherzo theme in Beethoven's *Archduke* Trio, op. 97; also the Scherzo of Schubert's posthumous Sonata in B flat.

[1] Schnabel liked to analyse this theme as consisting of 3+4+5 bars.

Example 70

Three-bar periods, especially in fast tempi, are very similar to ¾ bars.[1] The first two bars combined form the heavy part of the unit; the third bar the light. This is true of the end of the main section of Schubert's Impromptu in E flat, op. 90 no. 2. (Three-bar periods continue through to the end of the section, cf. also Ex. 149.)

Example 71

Five-bar and seven-bar periods, etc. are combinations of twos and threes and must be articulated with this in mind. According to Schnabel, the second half of the rondo theme in Beethoven's Fourth Piano Concerto must be understood as a seven-bar theme (the fifth to seventh bars being orchestral echoes of the fourth). As he performs the pianist must remember that the bars following, played by the orchestra, also belong to this metric unit. He should also be aware that harmony changes exist within every bar, which removes much of the natural weight of the down-beat. This is especially important in bar 4 where the half-cadence is completed only on the second beat, at which point the pianist tosses the music to the orchestra for the echoing bars.

[1] Beethoven's *ritmo di tre battute* marking in the Scherzo of the Ninth Symphony requests the conductor to beat three for each three bars as though they formed *one* ¾ bar.

65

CHAPTER SEVEN

Rhythmic Articulation

Rhythmic articulation has nothing to do with playing in time. As explained at the beginning of the preceding chapter, its goal is to make each rhythmic pattern audible as such – this includes separating it from its neighbours. This separation will be sharper in dance or other playful pieces than in lyrical melodies, but the principle of articulateness in the presentation of rhythms remains the same.

According to Schnabel, its realization depends partly on the ability to make a group of notes sound faster or slower at will, without changing the tempo. As an example, suppose that a pianist begins Beethoven's Sonata in F, op. 54 at exactly the same speed as the C minor Impromptu of Schubert, op. 90 no. 1.

Example 72a

Example 72b

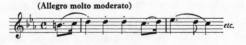

In this case the dotted rhythm of the first three notes will most probably sound slower in the Beethoven than in the Schubert, because the playing will tend to be fuller and more sustained.

Schnabel referred to this phenomenon as an 'acoustical illusion'–
parallel to an optical illusion–and deliberately used it as a means of
rhythmic clarification.[1] To this effect, he operated with dynamic
subtleties as well as with minute shadings of *legato*, *non-legato*, and
staccato, plus (if necessary) slight liberties in timing, i.e. *rubato*;
always in such a way that each note came at its appropriate time and
was held for its appropriate length, and each unit was heard as
rolling off at its ideal inner speed–all this without changing the
central tempo. But the most obvious tool for the performer is his
free use of punctuation (as it has been called since Türk's time),[2]
that is, of pauses for breathing in the melody, whether this is indicated in the score–by pauses; *tenuto*; commas, etc.–or not. In
Schumann's Sonata in G minor, op. 22, Schnabel, for instance,
would ask his students to pause and listen to the chord in bar 29
of the slow movement before going on:

Example 73

Likewise, in the second subject of the final rondo of Mozart's Piano
Concerto in D, K.451, as in many similar instances, he would
suggest inserting a comma after the third quaver in bars 2 and 3:

Example 74

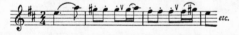

[1] Composers sometimes exploit this illusion by writing '*istesso tempo*' for
contrasting sections. The Finale of Beethoven's First Sonata and the slow
movement of Mozart's Concerto in D minor are famous examples. Schnabel
insisted that the effect only comes off if *exactly* the same tempo is used for the
main section as for the middle section in these movements.

[2] D. G. Türk, *Klavierschule*, 1789, Ch. 6, Section 2, paragraphs 17 ff.

This passage gains in 'playfulness' if, like Schnabel, the pianist plays each group a little too fast (although without an accent at the beginning of each phrase), making a 'Luftpause' before beginning the next group. Schnabel, though he was frequently criticized for it, applied this method in concerto playing wherever it would serve to clarify the structure. By playing the following example from Beethoven's Fourth Piano Concerto in this way he articulated the process of fragmentation.

Example 76

At first the short chords played by the orchestra occur in every other bar, then in every bar, and finally in every half-bar. Each time Beethoven marks a *forte*. The arpeggios in the piano part are subservient to the orchestral rhythm and fill the space following each chord. The rhythmic articulation as indicated depends on the *early beginning* of the right hand, so that there is no gap between the chord and the so-called 'fill-up' music. Schnabel observed this same principle in various other instances, such as the Finale of Schubert's Sonata in A minor, op. 42, A major section, bar 18,

Example 77

and in the slow movement of the *Waldstein* Sonata.

Example 78

Each time the 'fill-up' music starts at once. The same principle applies to the beginning of the coda of Chopin's Second Ballade—the second semiquaver to be played as early as possible.

In using free rhythmic nuances of this kind, the pianist can easily develop mannerisms and stereotyped articulations. Schnabel always tried to guard against this, particularly in passages of even semiquavers such as are to be found in every Mozart concerto. In these passages there is often a danger of playing faster towards the end of each bar; a tendency Schnabel described as 'the magical attraction towards the bar line'. As an antidote, he recommended for practising purposes playing the last two notes of every bar relatively slowly and less *legato* than the others, and even with a slight *crescendo*. For the urge to 'drop out' at the end of a bar is such a strong one for most people that if they *think* of a *crescendo* here, they will just be able to play the notes *evenly*!

Schnabel's attitude towards *rubato*, like all his attitudes, was highly original. He was one of the very few teachers who actually 'taught' *rubato*. Like Mozart and Chopin he demanded an unbroken line in the accompanying hand.[1] Leon Fleisher, when he insists in his teaching that in most cases any new bass-note must be secured before the *rubato* begins, carries this idea of Schnabel's one step further. In the Adagio of Mozart's Fantasia in D minor, K.397, the bass E', in the beginning of the second bar, has to be played in time: the second quaver of this bar can then be a trifle late. The possibility of *rubato* playing depends on the firmness of the surrounding structure. Schnabel used *rubato* mainly to achieve his goal of 'severity without rigidity' in classical works. He once stated that the slow

---

[1] Usually the left; but sometimes a left-hand *rubato* is played while the right hand pauses (Schubert, *Moment Musical* no. 2, bar 31) or accompanies (Weber, **Sonata in D minor**, Finale, second subject).

movement of the *Italian Concerto* by Bach, because of its firmer bass structure, lends itself better to *rubato* playing than any Chopin nocturne. The choice of *rubato*, however, does not depend on any criterion of style, but solely on the performer's momentary need for clarification of a melodic line–which he may feel today, but not tomorrow. *Rubato*, Schnabel said, is a permission, never an order; and he spoke with contempt of Chopin players who feel duty-bound to change tempo and distort rhythms as part of a 'Chopin style'. Once the idea of *rubato* was settled and its general outlines determined, the details of execution were invented spontaneously at the last moment.[1]

It is a prime function of rhythmic articulation to suggest *movement*. For this reason nothing upset Schnabel more than an accent made on the first note of a fast piece, especially if this was an up-beat–e.g. in Beethoven's Sonata in B flat, op. 22. 'You don't begin a movement with a stop,' he would say. Much of each lesson was always spent in securing the immediate characterization–which includes the 'rhythmics'–of a piece in its first few bars. At times he resorted to fictional changes of metre in order to achieve the rhythmic articulation he wanted. In the opening of Schubert's posthumous Sonata in B flat he wanted to avoid any point of gravity prior to the second down-beat. Therefore he imagined (and asked his pupils to do likewise) the beginning written in $\frac{3}{2}$, as follows:

Example 79

However, during the course of the piece, he would change over to heavier up-beats. It is impossible to give general rules about when an up-beat ought to be heavy and when it ought to be light. One could perhaps say–with all due caution–that on the whole Schnabel played up-beats with many notes–as in a gavotte or in the rondo theme in Beethoven's Sonata in G, op. 31 no. 1–more lightly than one-note up-beats.

[1] See p. 20.

Example 80

Rhythmic articulation, and its needs, was also what influenced Schnabel's selection of *tempo* more than any other single consideration. He did not believe that the exact fixation of tempo was a primary interpretive task. He believed, rather, that elasticity as well as spontaneity should, from one performance to the next, determine the tempo to some extent. He made fun of the many conductors who fight over minute differences in metronomic tempi.[1] In slow movements Schnabel tried to play as slowly as possible – he explained that the difficulty, contrary to what happens in *presto* music, increases with decreasing speed – without ever losing the tension between successive notes or the coherence of harmonic progressions. How often he would shout: 'Take your time!' His recording of the Larghetto from Mozart's last Piano Concerto, K.595, shows his faculty of stretching phrases in this way. On the other hand, his *allegretto* tempo was usually faster than most, because the rhythmic articulation here is light.

In short, one may sum up rhythmic articulation by saying that there is no characterization without freedom of timing, but that the long line of the music must never be disturbed.

[1] The greatest of them all once criticized Schnabel during an interval for just having played the opening of the *Hammerklavier* Sonata at $\bd = 132$ instead of 138! Schnabel liked to quote this as an example of the professional deformation of conductors' minds.

CHAPTER EIGHT

Score-Reading

(i) MARKINGS

1. *In general.* Difficulties in score-reading are usually under-estimated. Written notes are in themselves merely translations of sound into something visible. The visual translation can only give an approximate picture, for in the process of translating something is always lost. It fulfils its purpose when it is translated back into sound. Even so-called 'music for the eye' is just as much music for the ear as any other, although the eye may be helpful in preparing the ear for the sound. The true meaning of notation is not apparent until the spirit of the work is apprehended, for what is written down is only comprehensible in connection with what cannot adequately be expressed by the symbols of musical notation. The interpreter has two tasks which are inseparable. He must absorb the score as it is, and he must try to perceive the composer's *idea* behind it.

One fundamental rule for score-reading is that it must be *unbiased*. This is especially true of a score which has been heard or played many times before. Almost always the interpreter will make important discoveries in reading 'with renewed curiosity'. If at all possible the original text should be read. It is the surest way of stimulating the impulse to reproduction in the interpreter.[1] When the original is not available, as many editions as possible should be compared. Only then is it advisable for the performer to become acquainted with the traditional interpretation of the work, through critical editions or with the help of a teacher. In cases where the traditional interpretation is at variance with the expressed intentions of the composer, the performer must have the courage to go against tradition. It has

[1] See p. 120.

happened much more often than one would easily believe that the composer's personal friends and pupils were the first to falsify his intentions. The music of Chopin is one such instance. It shows the difficulty in ascertaining the final intentions of the composer beyond doubt. Chopin himself made alterations; some were added by others. Today it is almost impossible to arrive at the truth.

In the course of musical history, notation has on the whole become increasingly refined. Composers frequently aim at fixing even the most delicate nuances. Compare, for instance, the original score of a Bach fugue, which only has occasional indications of phrasing, with the almost cabalistic aspect of a score by Reger.

No doubt the composer's distrust of the interpreter, which grew stronger during the nineteenth century, played a part in this development. Schnabel believed that the increasing number of instructions in Beethoven's later works was a sign of growing scepticism about his interpreters. (The beginning of the last movement of the Sonata, op. 110, is very typical of this: see the footnote in Schnabel's edition.) Many of his more frequent indications take the form of warnings: *allegro ma non troppo*, *sempre pp*, etc. Schnabel considered the *con amabilità* at the beginning of op. 110 as a warning against 'thick' tone; the *semplice* in the second movement of op. 111 as a cautioning against excessive *rubato*. The pianist should have a general idea about the comprehensiveness of the markings of a score. In some of Mozart's sonatas the dynamic indications are complete, while in others (the Finale of K.570, for instance) only the unexpected *pianos* and *fortes* were notated. Some have no dynamic markings at all. Despite his awareness and knowledge of practice in performing, Schnabel tried to avoid putting an exaggerated value on any embellishment rules established by the musicologists.[1]

Apart from general variations and developments in notation,[2] there are individual differences in the markings of each composer.

[1] See p. 103f.

[2] Kullak, in 1861, was surprised at Türk's rule (1789) to play everything which is not slurred *non-legato*. In the meantime, through Czerny and others, the opposite rule had been established: all was to be *legato* that was not differently marked.

They all have their own habits and language which can only be learned by studying the different works of each one. What Beethoven means by *espressivo* can best be ascertained by comparing, for instance, the Finale of the *Waldstein* Sonata, bar 257; the Sonata, op. 109, third movement, first variation; the Sonata *Les Adieux*, first movement,[1] bar 34 of the Allegro; the Finale of the *Archduke* Trio, bars 5–6, etc. In these and in similar cases it appears that Beethoven intended the *espressivo* passages to be played with more tone than their surrounding passages. In this respect *espressivo* is opposed to *dolce*, and, with some exceptions, Beethoven usually avoids using the two terms together. Not all composers are equally adept at writing down their intentions. Beethoven was probably the greatest master of notation.[2] All his later works are written down with an astonishing skill of transcribing extreme subtleties of invention. Two favourite examples of Schnabel's to illustrate this are: (1) *Waldstein* Sonata Finale, bar 57. On the second beat, Beethoven adds a trill sign to the melody note G″, although a trill on the same note in *another* part had already been established two bars earlier. The trill is now, therefore, a double trill in unison, that is, for the duration of this beat it must be played twice as loudly. (2) Sonata in E, op. 109, variation theme, bar 6. The *gruppetto* in small notes is written in complex rhythms, suggesting the way in which it ought to be played *rubato*.

Schnabel did not confine his interest in notation to Beethoven. For instance, he spent considerable time in lessons in trying to explain some of Schumann's curious notational habits, such as writing the end note of a phrase as a grace-note wherever a new phrase would start in another part at the same time.[3] Examples of Schumann's notation technique will be discussed later.

[1] Schnabel felt that the *espressivo* marking referred only to the first three bars, that is, to the three notes of the main motive. See Ex. 34, p. 45.

[2] In Schnabel's opinion, people draw the wrong conclusion from Beethoven's illegible handwriting. Actually he was pedantic, as his German translations (like *geschliffen*) show; see also his tempo markings (in two languages) for variation 4 of the Sonata in E, op. 109, with academic definitions of *andante* and *adagio*.

[3] See Ex. 84.

2. *Reading of markings in general.* Schnabel insisted that, first of all, a student had to be clear whether a mark was by nature *strict* or not. The pitch indications, which and how many notes to play, except for certain embellishments, *tremolos*, etc., are completely strict. On the contrary, the marking *cantabile* is entirely elastic and appeals to the individual imagination of each performer. Between these extremes there are those markings which are *relatively precise,* as they establish a precise relationship to the neighbouring marks of the same category. To this category belong dynamic, tempo, *staccato* and other similar marks. Three of the four melody notes of the third bar of the second subject in Beethoven's Third Piano Concerto, first movement, are marked *portamento.*

Example 81

This does not establish exactly how long each is to be held, but it does establish that they must all have exactly the same length. (The tendency here is to play the third beat longer—and also louder—than the two others.) A *staccato* quaver must be shorter than a neighbouring *staccato* crotchet.[1] A good example of this is to be found at the beginning of the *Waldstein* Sonata. On the third beat of bar 3 the right hand plays a *staccato* quaver and on the third beat of bar 4 a *staccato* crotchet. The reason for the differentiation (which is carried out consistently throughout the movement) lies in the differing structure of the two phrases. The phrase of bar 3 has its weight at the beginning; the phrase of bar 4 at the end. Therefore the beginning of bar 4 should not be accented.[2]

Example 82

[1] See C. P. E. Bach, op. cit., I, Ch. 3, paragraph 17.
[2] See also Beethoven's Fourth Piano Concerto, Finale, bars 475, 477, 479, and 481.

In the same way dynamic markings are only relatively precise. A *piano* may be played in varying degrees of softness, but it must in any case be louder than a preceding or following *pianissimo*. In the Finale of Beethoven's Sonata, op. 110, two bars before the beginning of the first Arioso, the *piano tutte le corde* must sound very loud in comparison with the preceding bars.

Similar observations apply to indications of tempo. Although the performer has a certain amount of liberty in selecting the tempo, he should definitely respect the relationship of one tempo to another within the same piece or movement. Thus, the introduction to the third movement of Mendelssohn's Concerto in G minor (marked *Presto*) certainly must be played noticeably faster than the third movement itself (marked *Molto Allegro e vivace*).

Indications are often quite incomplete and call for a reasonable construction on the part of the reader. In bar 33 of the second movement of Beethoven's Sonata, op. 109 we find the notation *a tempo*. But this passage is preceded neither by a *ritardando* nor a *meno presto*. We are then entitled to conclude that the marking four bars earlier, *un poco espressivo*, also implies the term *un poco meno presto*. However we must not assume that it means *ritardando*. All four bars must be played in the same tempo. In the first piece of the *Davidsbündler*, Schumann gives no other tempo indication than *Lebhaft* and a single metronome marking for the whole movement. In view of the fact that Schumann was always very liberal with his directions, this can only mean that the first four bars are to be played in exactly the same tempo as what follows, that is, faster than is usually done.

To understand dynamic and tempo markings Schnabel thought it helpful for the pianist to ask himself how he would play the work if there were no marks at all. At the very beginning of Beethoven's Sonata, op. 111 for instance, one would certainly play *fortissimo* if Beethoven had not marked *forte*. Consequently the *forte* here carries with it the implication 'not too loud'. When Beethoven at the end of the Sonata, op. 109 marks *cantabile* for the recapitulation of the theme, he probably means 'not *mezza voce*'. The more unexpected an indication, the more weight it should carry.

At the same time it is part of the artist's task not to interpret the composer's instructions too widely. The temptation to do so is often great. A passage marked *presto* does not mean *prestissimo* nor does a *poco ritardando* justify a *molto ritardando*. A *fermata* does not automatically indicate a complete stop. Schnabel occasionally explained the length of a *fermata* by instructing the student to 'stop and listen, then go on'. A *fortissimo* does not imply a bombastic tone.

Instructions are often capable of more than one interpretation. The true meaning of the marking cannot be discovered by abstract reasoning. If a single dynamic marking is given for an entire lengthy section, it may mean that the section is to be played totally without dynamic shadings. It may mean, however, that the composer left it to the interpreter to introduce slight *crescendi* and *decrescendi*. In dubious cases it may as a rule be assumed that *piano* means *sempre piano*, and *forte*, *sempre forte*. This is especially true in Beethoven. In Beethoven's later works it is quite common for long passages to continue without any dynamic nuances, enlivened only by the articulation.

There is some disagreement as to whether *crescendi* and *diminuendi* are permissible in Bach's works, although Bach, in his keyboard works, does not prescribe them. Schnabel had strong reservations on the subject of what Schweitzer called 'terrace dynamics', i.e. juxtaposition of loud and soft sections. In the first place he objected to Schweitzer's image by saying: '*forte* and *piano* are at the same altitude, next to one another and not one on top of the other'. The idea seemed 'unmusical' to him inasmuch as 'music is essentially modulation, i.e. evolution'. Only in final cadences would Schweitzer's advice perhaps sometimes be acceptable. Finally, the whole idea of terrace dynamics, if at all applicable, certainly only fits one type of Bach's works, and even there, 'exceptions are fully admissible and desirable'.

In Mozart, it occasionally happens that a *crescendo* is indicated to bridge loud and soft passages, and certainly a *diminuendo*. The coda sections of some of his concertos (e.g. K.450 in B flat and K.467 in C) are marked *piano* in the orchestral parts, followed by *forte* in the last few bars. The solo parts have no dynamic markings. Whereas most soloists here operate by way of a gradual *crescendo*, Schnabel, conversely, played *diminuendo* so that the end would emerge in a sudden *forte*. The marking *fp* in Mozart means a small accent, but the marking is ambiguous. It can mean: first loud then soft; or else it can mean that only *some* of the notes forming a chord are to be played *forte*, while the others are to be played *piano*. In the beginning of the development of the Sonata in D, K.311, for instance, the *fp* marking refers primarily to the left hand.

Example 83

True, it is marked for both hands, but that does not mean that it must be *equally* loud in both and Schnabel was sure that the two parts played by the right hand—one just beginning, one just ending—could not tolerate much of an accent. Among other reasons, the first note of the imitation cannot be *forte*, if the original was *piano*.[1]

3. *Tempo marks*. They, too, are often incomplete. The Trio of a minuet or Scherzo rarely has a separate indication, but it may well be meant to be slower than the main section. Again, in some cases the absence of a marking indicates that both sections are to be performed at the same speed. The pianist has to rely on his musical instinct. Though not an infallible one, it is the only guide. The same goes for speed changes from one variation to the next. They may be justified in the absence of contrary indications. The shorter the theme, however—as for example in Beethoven's C minor Variations—the slighter the possibility of varying the tempo. The feeling of one central tempo for the entire work must be maintained, especially when a composer increases the motion from one variation to the next, as Beethoven does both in the *Appassionata*, op. 57, and in the Sonata in C minor, op. 111. One additional consideration, in sets of variations, was quite important to Schnabel: to plan rests and waits of varying length between each two variations. Most classical scores leave the choice of how much to separate successive variations to the performer.

[1] Schnabel's solution is questionable, because without a *forte* on C″ the dissonance between B and C″ cannot be clearly heard (see p. 45). I doubt that he would have used this interpretation in an actual performance.

Schnabel requested that the length of time between variations be worked out in advance and in a way allowing for differentiations: some variations follow immediately; some after a brief pause; some after a long fermata.

Metronome marks, too, are less unambiguous than one might think. They may be meant for the opening or for the further development. Schnabel always checked *all* sections of a score against the metronome mark. The marks may be given as hints (expressly so in Schoenberg's Five Piano Pieces, op. 23), or warnings. If Schumann marked the first movement of his Concerto as ♩ = 84 he knew that no pianist would want to carry this out.[1] Schnabel explained it as a warning: 'This should not be played too slowly'. But, on the other hand, he took Beethoven's metronome markings in op. 106 (*Hammerklavier* Sonata) most literally – if not bar for bar, at least as a general indication – because this is the only piano sonata carrying metronome marks, and because they are again, for the most part, exceptional in character: without them nobody would strive for such a fast tempo as Beethoven prescribes for the first and last movements.[2]

4. *Other markings. Staccato markings* may of course be heavy or light. Composers sometimes distinguish between dashes (heavy) and dots (light). In the absence of any such distinction the pianist must use his experience, knowledge and intuition to find out what the composer has in mind.

The notation of *grace notes* can be misleading. Schumann tends to write the last notes of phrases as though they were introductory to the next phrase (as stated earlier), for instance Fantasy, op. 17, Finale:

Example 84

(Ped. Ped.)

[1]Cf. Alan Walker, *Schumann*, London 1976, p. 48ff., on the subject of his metronome marks.

[2]To the frequent argument (Busoni, Tovey, etc.) that Beethoven was deaf when he marked the metronome speed here, Schnabel replied: 'But he was not blind!'

(Cf. *Kreisleriana* no. 4, bar 4, bass.[1]) In Ex. 84, the pseudo grace notes belong entirely to the previous phrase. Schumann chose this particular notation because he wanted the beginning of the following phrase to grow out of the final chord of the previous one. To this effect, the notes in small print must be much louder than the chord that follows. Also, one has to wait for a bit between the two, for the bass of the second chord—a first inversion of F major—is the note A, and not the low F. For the same reason, the pedal must be changed between the chord in small print and the inverted chord.

A *slur* may mean that the notes so indicated are to be played *legato*, but it may in addition indicate the length of the phrase.[2] In Mozart's works and the early works of Beethoven, this distinction is not always easy to make. When the slur reaches from the first to the last note of a bar, it probably does not prescribe the phrasing. Mozart is usually reluctant to let his slurs overlap the bar-line. There are, of course, exceptions. The Finale of his Sonata in C minor, K.457, is mostly conceived in double bars and the slurs in the bass therefore frequently extend over two bars:

Example 85a

and

Example 85b

Signs indicating *accents* (including the *sforzato* mark) may refer to a structural accent, or to an emphasis in articulation. In addition, accents are often used to emphasize a special rhythm, as is found

[1] See also Beethoven, Sonatina in G major, op. 49 no. 2, first movement, bars 36 and 40.

[2] But not shortening of the last note under a slur covering more than two notes. See Brahms's ambiguous letter to Joachim of May 30, 1879: 'to do so in longer groups of notes would be a liberty and nuance of interpretation which however is indicated in a majority of cases' (!).

especially in Schubert's works. Schnabel referred to these as 'accents of intensity', not unlike the prick of a needle, a slight emphasis given *subito*—without leading up to it—and disappearing just as suddenly. Cf. Schubert, Impromptu in B flat major, op. 142 no. 3, var. 2

Example 86

and Mozart, Sonata in C major, K.330, Finale.[1]

Example 87

Here the first of the two accents should be lightly supported by the left hand. Cf. also Beethoven, Sonata in A major, op. 2 no. 2, Finale:

Example 88

The accent is marked *sforzato* and thus is quite sharp, yet meant only as an accent of intensity. Most accents, in classical music, have the same quality as an increased *vibrato* produces on stringed instruments, and they are not meant to be at all percussive. Hence, in every case where an accent or a *sforzato* is used the musician must ask himself whether the mark refers to the entire chord or only to some of its parts. Even in the latter case there always remains a minimum of interdependence, if only for reasons of sonority. In the Trio of the Scherzo of Schubert's posthumous Sonata in B flat, every other bass note carries a *sforzato* mark. Schnabel insisted that to

[1] The marking *mfp* is to be found in the first edition which was authorized by Mozart, and is not in the manuscript.

clarify the syncopated character of the melody the right-hand note preceding each *sforzato* bass must also be accented.[1]

Example 89

In the Trio of Schubert's Impromptu in E flat, op. 90 no. 2, he requested the student to carry the left-hand accents on the second beat of many bars into the broken chords of the right hand,

Example 90a

corresponding to the actual texture.

Example 90b

This brings out the *vibrato* quality of the accent.

The first chord of Schumann's Fantasy, op. 17, is a ninth-chord implied by the first two notes (bass and ninth) in the left hand. The ninth must be played immediately so as to make the harmony clear as in a broken chord, and it must also be included in the *sf* marked for the bass.

[1] See Ex. 200.

5. *Pedalling instructions* by the composer may have one of two meanings. Either, as Schnabel formulated it, the pedal is a 'musical pedal' and belongs to the structure itself, or it is an 'instrumental pedal' and is intended only as a suggestion for tone colour. Schumann's pedal markings are usually of the latter kind. For the most part, he marks *Pedal* at the beginning of a piece and leaves it to the performer to decide how it should be used. Consequently, it is important to be aware of the passages that do not contain this instruction. In the fifth movement of *Kreisleriana* Schumann has marked the pedal only in the fifth bar, indicating beyond doubt that the first four are to be played without. Beethoven's rare pedalling instructions are without exception essential to the musical structure and do not leave any liberty to the performer. Nearly all these passages extend over changing harmonies, and the indicated pedalling produces a sound effect quite unusual in classical music. Editors and performers of Beethoven, frequently disturbed by this sound, have been known to disobey his orders and change the pedal with every change of harmony. The argument they have used is that in Beethoven's time, the pedal allegedly did not have the same effect since the piano tone was less lingering. But, according to Schnabel's evidence (which he asked me to include here) a trial carried out on a genuine Beethoven piano showed him that the pedal effect was as blurring as on a modern concert grand. Careful reading of the score proves that the pedalling must definitely be carried out exactly as prescribed and that in every case there is a valid musical reason for doing so. This applies to all of the most striking of Beethoven's pedalling instructions, such as the first movement recitatives of the Sonata, op. 31 no. 2, the second movement of the Third Piano Concerto, the Finale of the *Waldstein* Sonata, the second subject in the Finale of the Fourth Piano Concerto, and the coda of the Bagatelle, op. 126 no. 3. Schnabel believed that the musical idea in these passages was that the 'bass note must be audible until the next bass note is played'.[1] If the pianist chooses the appropriate tone proportion and tone colour, there will be no disturbing confusion in sound.

---

[1] See the note in the Finale of the *Waldstein* Sonata, Schnabel's edition.

The case of the recitatives in the first movement of the Sonata, op. 31 no. 2, is particularly instructive. The Largo is introduced by a dominant-sixth chord. The same chord opens the ensuing Allegro. If the pedal is held down during the entire recitative as Beethoven requires, there remains only a brief rest before the repeat of this chord at the start of the Allegro. Although the melody of the recitative ends on F, the dominant harmony is not resolved into the tonic chord of D minor, but co-exists with it. A comparison of this passage with the very beginning of the movement makes it absolutely clear that Beethoven wanted the dominant chord to sound as long as possible. For this reason the pedal should be continued to the end of the last note of the recitative. Schnabel also pointed to the identity of the last three notes of the first recitative with the first four of the following Allegro. The Allegro following the second recitative opens on a chromatic alteration of the underlying chord, while in the top part A flat' is enharmonically changed into G sharp'.

(ii) MUSICAL PENETRATION THROUGH SCORE-READING

Eye and ear work in such close collaboration that it hardly matters whether musical detail is first seen or heard. The eye either makes the discovery, and the ear checks it; or vice versa. Both phases of the working process are so inseparable that Schnabel could say: 'The musician sees with his ears and hears with his eyes.' In playing the first two bars of Schubert's posthumous Sonata in B flat, for instance,

Example 91a

the pianist may hear that—on top of a B flat pedal point in the bass—
the music is somehow held together by the dominant note in the
inner parts. His eye will then show him exactly how this comes
about: F and F′ are alternately played in the two hands, establishing
a quaver movement. Once seen, this movement becomes clear
enough to the ear and can be discreetly brought out:

Example 91b

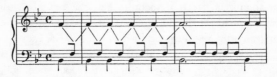

Obviously, if reading a score becomes an intense artistic activity, it
also creates problems of various kinds. In what follows we shall pick
out a few of these, in the same order and division by musical
elements which we observed in the earlier chapters.

1. *Reading melodic lines.* The pianist must guard against reading
two melodies as one, or reading notes into a melody which do not
belong there. In Schumann's Fantasy, op. 17, third movement,
bar 17 f.:

Example 92

the repeated top G″ in the right hand stands by itself and is not part
of the melody. In Mozart's Sonata in C minor, K.457, first movement, bar 95 f. (just preceding the recapitulation), and in Schubert's
Wanderer Fantasy, first movement, bar 20, the final chord each
time is not part of the melody, and only represents a pause filled
by an echo.

The opposite may also be the case, i.e., two parts may complete each other in forming a single melody. This happens frequently in Bach. Schnabel demonstrated it once in the Fugue of the Chromatic Fantasia and Fugue, bars 118/119:

Example 93a

This phrase must be played exactly as though Bach had written:

Example 93b

The very next bar confirms this:

Example 93c

Here the same music is written all in one part.[1]

Difficulties in the reading of melodies also arise through apparent rhythmic complications suggested by the notation. The following passage from Schumann's Sonata in G minor, first movement, is much simpler than it looks (bars 24 ff.):

Example 94a

[1] Many other examples of the same notation procedure can be found. I am sure, for instance, that in bar 1 of the Allemande from Bach's Second English Suite, the G sharp' in the alto part is in reality part of the top line theme. For in the inversion, bar 13, it is incorporated into the top line. The result is that precisely the careful polyphonic hierarchy between the parts (see p. 159 below) which one must generally observe, would here lead to a wrong interpretation of the score.

Its visual aspect is complicated by the fact that Schumann wrote both the quavers and the semiquavers as though they were syncopations. Yet the semiquavers in the inner part are primarily notes belonging to a broken chord and as such do not anticipate (as syncopations would) the following beat. The following notation, while in no way altering the music, would therefore have been much simpler to read:

Example 94b

In the very fast tempo prescribed by Schumann, the left hand, even when it is played with complete accuracy, will sound approximately like this:

Example 94c

Incidentally, this is not the only case in which Schumann marks broken chords in a way that makes them appear to be something else. In his Fantasy, second movement, bars 22 ff., the figurations played by the right hand—as Schnabel very emphatically pointed out—look like a dotted rhythm, but are not meant as such. They represent broken chords of a particular kind, in which the two top notes are played a fraction of a second earlier than the bottom note, which holds the melody. Therefore the top notes must not sound like upbeats; the thumb, that is, must play softest. The dotted rhythm grows out of this figuration four bars later. See also Beethoven's Sonata in B flat, op. 22, Finale:

Example 95a

to be played approximately as follows:[1]

Example 95b

In part-writing each part must be followed clearly, whether it is located in the right-hand area, the left-hand area, or divided between both. In the latter case, much care must be applied to the smooth transition from hand to hand: the hand that takes over must guard against accents on the first note played.[2] Part-writing, as hardly needs saying, occurs everywhere in piano music, not just in canons, fugues, etc. In Schubert's piano music there are many passages which seem like transcriptions from string quartets: extreme care is needed in watching the respective length of each note; the smooth *legato* connection between successive notes of each part wherever required, etc. See the Sonata in G, op. 78, second movement, coda; Sonata in B major, Scherzo, bars 21–24 (Ex. 210, p. 177). Schnabel saw a major technical difficulty in learning these passages perfectly.

Preliminary to the reading of each part, of course, is the knowledge of how many parts there are. Surprisingly, this requirement is not always met. In the first theme of the Finale of Schubert's Sonata in A minor, op. 42, the two-part writing of the beginning is interrupted by one long G' in bar 7. By playing this note as an independent voice apart from the rest of the music, one creates the necessary space for this melody.

2. *Reading harmonies.* This becomes a problem when the harmonies are incomplete or hidden, as easily happens in scale passages.

---

[1] Schnabel has sometimes been criticized for supposedly sloppy technical playing when dealing with broken chord figurations in this manner, because his critics did not understand that there was a musical intention behind it, namely, to bring the melody out, and thus to avoid the mechanical sound of completely even figurations. 'I hear too many notes,' he would say when a pupil played that way, especially in broken octaves.

[2] Schubert, posthumous Sonata in B flat, first movement, bars 179, 187, 193, etc.: any accent on the first chord played by the hand that takes over would be absolutely fatal!

Take, for example, an extract from the end of the first movement of Beethoven's *Waldstein* Sonata, op. 53:

Example 96a

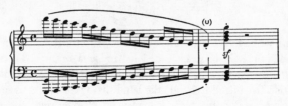

These bars are harmonically misunderstood if they are heard as one long dominant harmony. In reality, the harmonies are as in

Example 96b

which was approximately how Schnabel played the passage for his pupils in order to show them what their ears and eyes ought to read here. To make this harmonic structure clear, A on the third beat of bar 1 must be emphasized discreetly, and the second beat of bar 2 must be played a little late in order to sound as what it is: an anticipated, and therefore accented, up-beat to the next bar.

Blurred harmonies usually make the beginning of the final *stretto* in Brahms's First Piano Concerto very hard to follow. Schnabel not only emphasized the *upper* notes of each pair of notes, but he also separated each of these pairs, so that the passage

Example 97a

sounded like

Example 97b

or even

Example 97c

ma non legato!

This rhythmic licence is similar to what ought to happen in the opening theme of the Finale of Beethoven's Concerto in C–which Schnabel played exactly as Czerny[1] indicated that Beethoven himself played it.

Example 98a

Example 98b

Enharmonic changes and spelling subtleties are often a great help towards full understanding, and the pianist who studies a score must look for them with care. In the development section of the *Hammerklavier* Sonata, op. 106, first movement, Beethoven writes:

Example 99

The D″ with which the example begins, and which is repeated two bars later at the octave below, must not sound like a passing-note, otherwise Beethoven would have written C double-sharp″, as he does in bar 5 of the example. To manifest his intention of modulating from B minor to B major is possible by separating the two chords

---

[1] *Über den richtigen Vortrag . . .*, p. 107.

through lingering on the first, and stressing the second, both with extreme discretion.[1]

3. *Reading metrical particularities.* Just as Aristotle's unities of time, place and action governed drama, it seems that in the minds of composers the unities of metre, key and motive governed their musical works, not only in baroque, but still in classical times. The tonality was the 'place' of the music, the motive corresponded to the 'action' and the constant metre secured the unity of the 'time' element. Therefore the key and time signatures were, as a rule, unchanging throughout each piece. There is, however, this difference between the two signatures: it does not need a change of key signature to enlighten us in what key we are at the moment: our knowledge of harmony tells us that. The composer can therefore safely modulate without changing the key signature. But if he changes the metre without changing the time signature, he nearly always creates misunderstandings. It is an exception when the reader can at once identify the real metre, as in the coda of the slow movement of Schubert's Sonata in B, op. 147:

Example 100a

obviously meant as:

Example 100b

The performing musician will often be helped by thinking of a

[1] Charles Rosen, *The Classical Style,* New York, 1971, pp. 413-420, explains the structural importance of this detail.

change of metre in the cases of three-note arpeggios conflicting with a time signature of $\frac{4}{4}$, or vice versa. It was almost automatic that Schnabel, in these cases, would count according to the arpeggio division by octaves and not according to the signature, so that the same arpeggio-note would always come on the same beat of the bar. In the introduction to the Finale of Beethoven's *Les Adieux*, Schnabel did not count, as the signature would indicate:

Example 101a

(quoting the principal notes only)—but

Example 101b

The same procedure was adopted by Schnabel in Beethoven's *Polonaise*, op. 89, at the first interlude, corresponding to the implied chord pattern:

Example 102a

Example 102b

Brahms was extremely fond of surreptitiously changing the metre, and not all the places in which he did this can be solved in an unambiguous way. One of the simpler devices, which he constantly used as the baroque composers had done, was the substitution, in $\frac{3}{4}$ time, of one $\frac{3}{2}$ bar, in *hemiola* tradition, for two $\frac{3}{4}$ bars. For the performer this means that the metrical accents, if any, belong to the hidden, not to the apparent metre. The second movement of his Cello Sonata in

E minor starts on the second beat of a hidden $\frac{3}{2}$ bar; if the performers can hear it that way they will not accent the first apparent down-beat (D), but play to the second down-beat (A minor chord) without accent.

But most of Brahms's changes are difficult to unravel. Schnabel was convinced that Brahms deliberately challenged or teased his performers by not indicating in his time signatures what metre he had in mind. Some of Brahms's hidden changes of metre call for bold assumptions on the part of the performer. The Rhapsody in E flat, op. 119 no. 4, Brahms's last piano piece, is obviously not meant to be played in the simple $\frac{2}{4}$ metre in which Brahms wrote it down, thereby eliminating every problem.

Example 103a

Schnabel explained and taught the real metre as follows: two bars in $\frac{2}{4}$ followed by two bars in $\frac{3}{4}$; the same repeated twice; one bar in $\frac{3}{2}$ alternating with one in $\frac{2}{2}$; the same repeated four more times. The beginning, if written down according to its real time signature, would then look like this:

Example 103b

Certain features of the phrase structure are clarified in this assumption: bars 1–15 of the score become a twelve-bar period in which the last four bars form the last third of a symmetrical triptych, and not (as one might otherwise think) the beginning of a new section. The new section, indeed, begins only as the beat changes over to minims (from crotchets) in bar 16 of the score. Both the $\frac{2}{4}$–$\frac{3}{4}$, and the $\frac{3}{2}$–$\frac{2}{2}$ alternations amount to five minims each, which gives the music its metrical unity and special charm.

The performer who has learned to read in one metre what has been written in another, will sometimes use this skill (as was shown on p. 71) for better articulation. It was a favourite device, almost a game, in Schnabel's study of scores; and he applied it especially wherever an unaccompanied slow scale was used as a transitional 'tool' by composers; e.g. Beethoven, *Archduke* Trio, op. 97, second movement, coda:

Example 104a

where he played a *hemiola*:

Example 104b

Weber, *Invitation to the Dance*

Example 105a

(lusingando)

which he played in a more complex arrangement as 3+4+5 beats:

Example 105b

The main purpose and effect of these 'metre games' is to avoid down-beat accents in such exposed passages. They must not be stopped by interrupting accents, since their only function is to act as an unobtrusive transition.[1]

There are, of course, other kinds of examples. In the left hand of the recapitulation of the rondo theme in Beethoven's Sonata in G, op. 31 no. 1, Schnabel would ask for a 'waltz rhythm':

Example 106a

Example 106b

In the first trio of Brahm's Scherzo in E flat minor, op. 4, Schnabel marked in a pupil's score as shown below:

Example 107a

Example 107b

However, not every melody pattern which contradicts the given metre is necessarily meant in a different metre: sometimes the con-

[1] See p. 127.

tradition is supposed to be heard as such. The second theme of the Finale of Schumann's Piano Concerto, ostensibly in $\frac{3}{2}$, is not only written, but *meant* to be heard in a syncopated $\frac{3}{4}$. Schnabel requested conductors to beat $\frac{3}{4}$, and not $\frac{3}{2}$, for this passage (especially where the theme is played *tutti*). The *fortissimo* chords at the beginning of Beethoven's *Appassionata*, op. 57, are to be heard according to the time signature:

Example 108a

and not:

Example 108b

At the end of the introduction to Brahms's Second Concerto, bars 25–28, Schnabel combined a metre change from $\frac{4}{4}$ to $\frac{2}{2}$ (in other words, to *alla breve*) with an augmentation of the quaver triplets used in the preceding bar, and played the melody, as shown here in outline,

Example 109

in triplets, but so that—in these triplet values—a polyrhythmic pattern of $\frac{6}{4}$ (crotchet triplets) in the melody[1] against $\frac{3}{2}$ in the

---

[1]This passage corresponds to bars 115ff., after the first orchestral *tutti* in the *Emperor* Concerto, inasmuch as a scale motive is being accelerated from crotchets to crotchet triplets.

oscillating pedal point on F (minim triplets) supports the gradual increase in sound and tension of the music, in which the up-beat phrasing, as marked in our example, was important to Schnabel.

There are no general rules laying down in what places a performer can and should give in to the hidden metre change suggested by the composer, and in which he should resist this by adopting a syncopated rendering. The character of the music, as the performer understands it, has to decide. The example from the *Appassionata* calls for a maximum of rhythmic tension, hence Schnabel's reading. The coda of the slow movement of the Schubert Sonata must be played peacefully, hence the complete yielding to the suggested common time in the music (see Ex. 100).

Schnabel, without any effort, was perfect in polyrhythmic playing. In places like Beethoven's Polonaise, op. 89:

Example 110

and his Bagatelle, op. 119 no. 2, coda:

Example 111

you could hear the two-against-three of the two hands—in both these examples meant playfully—as if they had been played by two people. The same could be heard in the three-against-four passage of the Adagio of the *Emperor* Concerto, bar 48. He demanded the same kind of polyrhythm for bar 6 of variation 2 of Beethoven's *Eroica* Variations, op. 35; and for the B minor (*pp*) passage preceding the second theme in the *Emperor* Concerto, bar 151ff.

As all these examples show, Schnabel tried to find the inner time of the music regardless of the time signatures and bar lines he read in the score. He defined the function of a bar line as 'a simple traffic regulation, not a landscape'. I am sure he would have welcomed Thomas Heinitz's slogan: 'Bar lines, like little boys, should be seen but not heard.' He did not even want to see them: indeed he declared that, if he were rich enough, he would have all music printed for his personal use without bars and metres (as in the slow movement of Mendelssohn's early Piano Sonata in E)!

4. *Reading rhythms.* This includes the recognition of possible hidden rhythmic patterns behind a façade of quick even notes.[1] Schnabel sometimes heard the stereotyped three up-beat quavers of classical music in successions of even semiquavers. See Mozart, Piano Concerto in A, K.488, first movement, bar 86:

Example 112

Schubert, *Wanderer* Fantasy, slow movement, bar 18:

Example 113

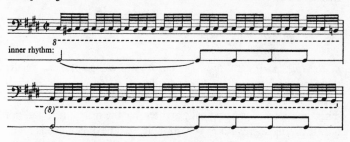

There will be other examples of this later on.

When sight-reading rhythms it is important to recognize the larger patterns which result from a repeat of obvious small patterns. Bach, for instance, as in the first counterpoint of the Chromatic

[1] See Ralph Kirkpatrick, Preface to Bach's *Goldberg* Variations, Schirmer Edition, p. xxiv.

Fugue, likes to group three pairs of two semiquavers and one quaver into one overall rhythmic pattern: 'An-de-*two*; an-de-*three*, an-de-*one*'; the three form a single rhythmic figure. The authentic pedal extending over the first four bars of Beethoven's *Hammerklavier* Sonata was understood by Schnabel in the same way: the second two bars are meant not as a repeat but as a completion of the rhythmic motive.[1]

As explained earlier (see Ex. 54), rhythms must be read independently of the metre, that is, independently of the exact place at which they appear within the framework of bar lines; moreover, rhythms must be recognized when they are quoted in diminution or augmentation. Schnabel called attention, for instance, to the up-beat rhythm in the bass which introduces the B minor episode in the Finale of Mozart's Sonata in D, K.311:

Example 114a

(bar 118) and is quoted later (bar 126) at double speed.

Example 114b

5. *Reading particular tone effects.* Many composers, especially those of the last century, occasionally strive for unpianistic tonal effects such as *vibrato*, *pizzicato*, or *crescendo* on a sustained note. This occurs in pieces originally written for the instrument and not only in arrangements from orchestral pieces. The difficult coda of the second movement of Schumann's Fantasy belongs to this category. As in the beginning of the movement, there is no dotted rhythm proper to be read into the score, rather a series of arpeggios (each of which consists of six notes) implying a *pizzicato* effect. This can be

---

[1] It seems to me that the beginning of the Sonata in E flat, op. 7, ought to be pedalled and played in the same way, being the same kind of pattern, though played softly at first.

attained by playing the inner notes most loudly, that is, by making a *decrescendo* towards the top and bottom.[1]

Example 115

Arpeggio-type figurations are often meant as a substitute for an orchestral *tremolo*–for instance the beginning of Brahms's Cello Sonata in F, op. 99.

A classic example of a *vibrato* imitation occurs in the middle section of Schubert's Impromptu in E flat, op. 90 no. 2 (see Ex. 90 on p. 83). The accent on the second beat in the left hand is undoubtedly meant as a *vibrato* accent. It is completed by the simultaneous figuration in the right hand. The accent should not be too strong. A real *vibrato*, of course, is impossible on the piano.

A *crescendo on a held note* can be simulated and, to some extent, actually achieved by a *crescendo* in a lower part: e.g. the opening of Mozart's Sonata in B flat, K.333:

Example 116

A slight increase in the left-hand melody towards the third beat of bar 2 suggests and produces a reinforcement of the long E flat″ in the right hand.

---

[1] Schnabel advised his student to bend thumb and index finger in each hand into a ring while striking the inner notes.

CHAPTER NINE

Accuracy of Execution

Schnabel believed that in artistic activity accuracy is the result of penetration of the spirit rather than of scholarly endeavour. He claimed that those pianists who tried to double as musicologists by stem-splitting looks at the score with a magnifying glass were more apt to make mistakes about notes, phrasing, etc. than those who, using the best available edition and reading it carefully, would afterwards just concentrate on what the composer had in mind (e.g. the right-hand *pp* in Ex. 186 below may be overlooked, unless the reader understands the metrical structure). The 'philologists', as he pejoratively called those obsessed with the mini-problems of score-reading, think of accuracy as a goal for the interpreter. But in reality this can never be: accuracy has an entirely negative value, 'like not stealing silver spoons'.

As stated in the last chapter, the performer must distinguish between the *essentials* and the *secondary* indications in the scores written by composers.

(i) ESSENTIALS

1. Here belong the *notes themselves* which, even in fantasies and cadenzas, must be rendered without changes, cuts or additions.[1] According to A. W. Thayer's Life of Beethoven,[2] Czerny in 1816 permitted himself certain alterations, such as adding passage work and using higher octaves, while playing Beethoven's Piano Quintet,

---

[1] He never 'filled' anything in Mozart concertos that was not so ordered in the score. Cf. about this controversial question: Eva Badura-Skoda, *Mozart Jahrbuch 1957*, 186.

[2] Ed. Forbes, 1964, vol. II, p. 640.

op. 16–composed twenty years earlier–and was severely reprimanded by Beethoven in the presence of other performers. Beethoven, in a letter written the next day, reiterated that as 'a composer . . . [he] would have preferred to hear his work exactly as he wrote it, no matter how beautifully you played in general'. In Bach's works Schnabel forbade any adding of octaves as not only inadmissible, but superfluous: when Bach wants them he writes them, as in the coda sections of the Fifth Partita and the Chromatic Fugue.

'Revised' and 'critical' editions usually make accuracy harder, not easier to achieve. In doubtful cases musical standards alone can give the answer.

2. *Embellishments and Figurations.* Except for *tremolos* proper (Weber, Sonata in A flat, opening) and trills, where the exact number of notes is not fixed, the pianist must play the exact number of notes the composer has written. This applies, for instance, to the 'Ghost' movement of the Beethoven Trio in D, op. 70 no. 2; to the middle section of his Funeral March in the Sonata in A flat, op. 26; and to the opening of Schubert's Fantasia for piano and violin in C.

Schnabel was not exceedingly interested in the exact details of embellishments in baroque music. For him, the most important factor in the performance of an embellishment was the preservation of its decorative character. This called for a certain amount of spontaneity. In a footnote to bar 32 of Beethoven's Sonata in A, op. 2 no. 2, Finale, his edition explains two possible ways in which to play the turn that occurs in this bar; then Schnabel adds: 'As for myself, I play this passage just as fancy strikes me, one way or the other.' Too much focusing on the mordent, turn, etc., draws the attention away from that which is being embellished; that is, from the content and character of the composition; the performance becomes, as Schnabel expressed it, one of 'a little music between trills'.[1]

[1] The same is true of literature: Carl Jaspers, *Die Geistige Situation der Zeit*, 1953, p. 105, says, of authors preoccupied with style and language: 'If I view scenery through a glass window, when the glass becomes dirty I can still see through it; but not any longer if I now focus my eye on the window itself.'

But Schnabel did not imply that a student should not consult the authorities on the correct execution of embellishments. For the purposes of this book, he referred the reader to C. P. E. Bach's *Versuch*; to Quantz's *Anweisung* . . . and, for later music, to Adolf Beyschlag's *Die Ornamentik der Musik* (1908). He only warned his students against automatic application of the solutions offered in these books as they tend to transform art into academic demonstration, and music into musicology.[1]

The principal melody note must always be more audible than the embellishment. Schnabel himself always played embellishing notes softer and more *leggiero* than the principal ones. This is how he wanted the second theme in the Finale of Beethoven's Concerto in G to begin:

Example 117

Only exceptionally, for harmonic reasons, would he accent a grace note (as in Schubert's Sonata in G major, op. 78, Minuet):

Example 118

But he often added, even then, that a grace note must always preserve that character and not become a 'disgrace note'.

It should be added that Schnabel avoided playing measured trills and turns exactly coinciding with the figurations of the left hand, in order to let the embellishment be heard as free of the pigeonholes

[1] In variation 19 of Brahms's *Handel* Variations he suggested playing the mordent on the beat in the lower voice, but later to play it before the beat when it becomes part of the top part melody.

awaiting each normal note, e.g. the theme of the *Romance* from Mozart's Piano Concerto in D minor, K.466:

Example 119a

and not:

Example 119b

3. *Length of Notes.* Mozart's music is one of the principal objects and victims of inaccuracy in this respect. Many pianists are inclined to hold notes too long, especially bass notes, and many tend to clip melody notes on which a phrase comes to an end. The holding over of bass notes, particularly in Alberti basses, is partly based on a tradition which started in the middle of the last century, and partly on lack of technical control as the fifth finger of the left hand does not easily come off the key it is holding down. (When Schnabel noticed this in lessons, he usually said: 'Lazy elbow.')

In Beethoven's music, the same inaccuracy mars performances of melodies which—as happens in variations—dissolve into slow figurations: See Sonata, op. 57, second movement, variation 2 and Schnabel's footnote;[1] Sonata, op. 26, first movement, variation 5. This slow and tender piece is written without any long notes. The prescribed *legato*, according to Schnabel, must be achieved without pedal and without accents, especially in the right hand. See also Schubert, Impromptu in A flat, op. 142 no. 2, Trio:

Example 120a

---

[1] In his Sonata edition Schnabel became a reformer by finally repudiating Bülow's outdated ideas, of which the arbitrary change in note values was one of the most offending to him.

and not

Example 120b

If this accuracy is thought to be exaggerated and pedantic, one must point out the instances in which Schubert himself *wants* a melody note held over (like other composers, including Bach before him). Schubert's purpose here was to create a pedal substitute, as in bars 26 and 28 of the Impromptu in E flat, op. 90 no. 2: here he himself writes these notes with a double stem.

One aspect of being accurate in the holding of melody notes is that this prevents any misunderstanding about the actual notes which form the melody. The beginning of the A major section in Schumann's *Novelette*, op. 21, no. 7, must clearly be heard as:

Example 121a

and not

Example 121b

The fourth bar of Schubert's posthumous Sonata in B flat should *not* sound:

Example 122

(cf. Ex. 79).

Both can only be achieved if the down-beat notes of the melody are held through. The best way of achieving melodic clarity, which Schnabel constantly recommended, is by practising the melody separately, without any accompaniment in the beginning, just as a singer or violinist would–until it sinks in; so that the inner ear can control its rendering at all times, even if the attention is wandering to some other part of the music for a moment.

The shortening of end notes of a phrase is a terrible habit which dates back many generations, when Mozart's music was considered mainly quaint and graceful. Again, it is his music which principally suffers from these inaccuracies. His variety of rhythmic presentation is incorporated in the varied length of accompanying notes, as at the beginning of the Concerto in C, K.467, bar 86:[1]

Example 123

A little later in the same movement (bar 110), the four notes composing a G minor chord in the left hand have different note values which must be heard clearly, which also means that the pedal has to change.

Example 124

Schnabel paid special attention to all left-hand parts in Mozart's works, especally the concertos. They must be free of accents and *staccato*: a left-hand *staccato* is very rare in Mozart. Crotchets, though not to be held over, must be held. And of course, end notes must not be abbreviated as though they were marked *staccato*. This applies especially to feminine endings like these (Sonata in D, K.311, first movement, end of coda):

[1] See also the left hand in variation 1 of the Sonata in D, K.284, Finale.

Example 125

N.B.   N.B.   N.B.   N.B.   N.B.

It is imperative, in particular, not to shorten the final chord of the piece.

Where, as in Ex. 123 above, bar 2, left hand, a crotchet chord is succeeded by a crotchet rest it is important, as Schnabel would explain and demonstrate, to release the three notes of the chord precisely together, which enhances the eloquence of the rest. Rests 'are not a vacuum'. Schnabel's mental association with the term was: 'Patience–body must pause.' This is also true for incomplete rests, as for instance, rests during which the pedal is held or one part pauses while another is sustained.

4. *Legato and staccato markings.* Wherever possible a complete finger *legato* should be used, even when the pedal is sustained at the same time. Schnabel considered this mandatory, for instance, in the performance of the opening theme of Beethoven's Sonata in E, op. 109, despite the technical difficulty caused by the fact that the upper notes in the first three bars have to be struck just beforehand.

Schnabel liked to demonstrate–although he considered it obvious–with the example of the rondo theme from Beethoven's *Waldstein* Sonata, that though the pedal is held, a note or chord can sound *staccato* (in this case, the second beat of bar 1) if thus played. The same is true for *portamento*, as in the opening of the slow movement of Beethoven's *Emperor* Concerto: if this is played correctly, the *portamento* will not be taken for a *legato* in spite of the sustained pedal.

The brilliant figurations in Mozart's concertos, which are sometimes given to the left hand as well, have to be played *legato*. This rule is practically without exception, since they are modelled on vocal *coloratura* and not on violinistic articulation. This, of course, does not inhibit their full melodic articulation depending on their direction, as discussed earlier.

In *staccato* sequences Schnabel pointed out the danger of playing the *staccato* notes louder or longer when they occur on down-beats. A good example of this would be the Finale theme of Mozart's 'easy' Sonata in C, K.545: its third note must not be prolonged or metrically accented in performance. In the Finale of Beethoven's Sonata in E flat, op. 27 no. 1, bars 12 and 13, Schnabel warned against interrupting the even *staccato* on the down-beats by accents:

Example 126

See also Ex. 81.

5. *Rhythmic Precision.* With very few exceptions, the rhythmic notation in a traditional score must be made understandable enough to the listener so that, if he is a musician, he would be able to write down (at least in essentials) the length of notes and rests, the metre, etc. with perfect accuracy. This precision can be attained in freely declaimed music as well as in works strictly played, as long as the performance permits a musician listener to identify the rhythmic notation in the score with a good deal of approximation. The quick notes following a dot, in so-called dotted rhythm, should not sound either like the end note of a triplet (as in jazz) or like double-dotting (as in some baroque music).[1] This applies in passages like Ex. 72 on p. 66.

As for rhythmic complexities, in case of doubt wherever possible Schnabel adopted a reading which permitted him to have more than one rhythm going on at the same time. In the slow movement of Mozart's Piano Concerto in C, K.467, he was strict about the co-existence of four semiquavers in the right hand with triplets in the left, and he would not permit his students to shorten the up-beat semiquavers in the first bar of the theme, from $\frac{1}{4}$ of the beat to $\frac{1}{6}$ (that is, half-way between two triplet notes): they had to have the

---

[1] The universal acceptance of double-dotting in Bach when a single dot is written, as in the beginning of his C minor Partita and many other places, is of too recent date to have been considered by Schnabel who, about 1948, recorded Bach's D major Fugue from Book I of the *Well-Tempered Clavier* without altering any of Bach's dots into double-dots.

exact same length as the four semiquavers at the end of the second bar. This means, they come right after the last note of the triplet is played. He adopted the same rhythmic interpretation in similar cases in Schubert: in the middle section of the slow movement of the posthumous Sonata in B flat, Schnabel played the demisemiquavers later than the last of each group of semiquaver triplet notes:[1]

Example 127

Even in Bach, though most of the time, if the beat is split three ways, the dotted rhythms in the other hand are attenuated in order to conform (as in the B flat major Partita, Courante),[2] there exist cases of undoubtedly genuine polyrhythm—for instance the Gavotte from the E minor Partita—which justify Schnabel's attitude. But Schnabel was aware that the opposition of rhythms in a two-against-three passage must sometimes be smoothed out rather than underlined. He then would think in triplets only and tell his students to count 'one—two—and—three—one . . .'. Two examples of this:

[1] I do not remember whether in the song *Die Wasserfluth* Schnabel played the semiquavers later than the last triplet notes. This case, which has been extensively discussed in recent years, is different from that of Ex. 127 because the triplets are located in the treble, so that a literal performance of the semiquavers would have the bass move in quicker note values than the melody:

Example 128

[2] Chopin uses the same notation, as in the last part of his *Polonaise-Fantaisie*.

Example 129a

(Brahms, D minor Concerto, first movement, bar 215)

to be thought of as

Example 129b

and

Example 130a

(Schubert, Sonata in B flat, first movement, bar 171)

to be thought of as

Example 130b

In this example, however, Schnabel asked for syncopated accents on the top notes played by the left hand, executed 'with loose thumbs'. Another aspect of rhythmic precision is discussed below, example 133.

6. *Accuracy of Dynamics.* As explained before, the quantity of sound cannot be defined in absolute categories–so many decibels for

forte; so many for *piano*–only in relation to the quantity of sound used just before and just after the passage under scrutiny.[1]

Schnabel constantly criticized his pupils for what he called 'internal dynamics', that is, nuances added to what the composer had marked where they would distort the line or over-emphasize some details at the expense of others. He particularly opposed the idea expressed in some of the older piano schools[2] that, as a matter of course, a *crescendo* should accompany a rise in pitch, and a *decrescendo* a fall. Although, as we have seen,[3] rises in pitch are important, a tune can be trivialized beyond repair if its ascending line is emphasized when this is clearly audible. For instance, no *crescendo* should lead up to the fourth bar of Schubert's Impromptu in A flat, op. 142 no. 2.

Example 131

Inconsistencies in the execution of *crescendos* and *diminuendos* also irritated Schnabel. In accordance with his principles of articulation, during a *crescendo* he would not admit any drop in loudness between beats, not even in the event of two-note phrasings. Thus, in bar 24 of Beethoven's Sonata in A flat, op. 110, he ruled out any *diminuendo* from the first to the second beat:

Example 132

[1] Brahms knew so well that *forte* indicates a quality, a character, rather than a sonorous quantity that–according to Diran Alexanian's report of what Brahms said to him–he defined his (frequently occurring) marks of *poco forte* as 'with the character of *forte*, but the sound of *piano*'.

[2] Czerny already mentions this in the last of his *Letters on Thorough Bass*; also Adolf Kullak *Aesthetik des Klavierspiels*, p. 537 ff.; Otto Klauwell *On Musical Execution* (translated from the German) p. 60; Malvine Brée *The Groundwork of the Leschetitzky Method* (1902, American ed. 1905), p. 65.

[3] See p. 36 f.

Wherever, in fast tempo, the character of the music was agitated, he would indeed concentrate his *crescendo* on the notes played *between* the beats: this gave these sections some moments of extraordinary intensity and excitement.

7. *Accuracy of Speed.* I refer, most of all, to the obligation to stick to the tempo once chosen, especially in the first and last movements of classical sonatas and concertos. This includes brilliant passages: in the recapitulation of the first movement of Beethoven's *Emperor* Concerto the composer's '*senza tempo*' mark comes only at bar 371, and Schnabel insisted that up to this point, that is, during bars 363–70, the solo passages have to be played in strict time. Special care for the preservation of the same tempo must be taken when a *new theme* or a *new rhythmic motion* sets it. The lyrical second themes of Mozart's Piano Concerto in A, K.488, first movement, and of Beethoven's *Waldstein* Sonata, first movement, may not be taken any slower than the opening of the movement; at least not noticeably so. For examples of a sudden change in motion, see the opening of the second half of the initial Adagio of Mozart's Sonata in E flat, K.282, and the recapitulation of his 'easy' Sonata in C, K. 545.

Sometimes there is a danger of playing short notes too fast when they are in juxtaposition with longer notes, or–which amounts to the same thing–longer notes too slowly when they alternate with shorter note values. For instance, Weber, *Invitation to the Dance*; *Vivace* section, bars 9–12:

Example 133

Here Schnabel helped his pupils by saying: 'Play fast quarter- and slow eighth-notes, if you want to play in time.' Another example is the Trio of Schubert's last *Moment Musical*, op. 94 no. 6, in which Schnabel called for slow quavers at the end of bars 1 and 2, and fast crotchets in bar 3.

Ritardandos should only be made where they are marked, and before a *fermata* (where in classical music this is nearly always implied). The same older piano schools quoted earlier mostly advise the contrary: *ritardandos* introducing deceptive cadences, recapitulations, etc. The great composers would have been horrified, as Schnabel was, by such false dramatics. The customary slowing-down at the end of Bach's compositions, however, can be justified as long as it does not interrupt the beat, which, though slowed down, must be felt to the very end. No *ritardando* should begin earlier than it is written. In the Schumann Concerto, when the theme appears in C major, Schnabel asked his students to play in strict time up to the harmonic cadence where a slowing-down is prescribed:

Example 134

After the end of passages played *senza tempo*, particularly in cadenzas, the pulse must deliberately be restored so that the continuity of the piece as a whole is, as it were, retroactively saved. The three soft chords which precede the orchestral *tutti* in the opening of Beethoven's *Emperor* Concerto belong to this species and must therefore be played most strictly (though *piano*) in time.[1]

In the same way, strict tempo is restored following a *ritardando*, a *fermata* and even a *rubato*, at the end of a metrical period–advice which Schnabel gave especially for the rendering of Chopin Mazurkas: he held that the common tendency to falter at the end of phrases runs counter to their very essence. Also, in the opening theme of the Schumann Concerto, the last one-and-a-half bars, following two syncopated bars, though light, must be strictly in time, in the interest of the balance of the phrase.

[1] Also bar 372; see also Brahms's Concerto in D minor, second movement, bar 44.

8. *Accuracy of phrasing.* Essential phrase marks are those which establish, in the ear of the listener, the identity of a motive, theme, or melody. Such a mark is the slur which connects the first two notes of the theme of Beethoven's Sonata in A flat, op. 110.

Example 135a   Example 135b

If this is not observed most transparently, the tune will be heard as having three (and not two) up-beat-notes A flat′ leading into the second bar; and it will not sound 'identical', as Schnabel expressed it, with what Beethoven wrote. In his famous Waltz in A flat, did Brahms quote from this theme?

Example 136

Whether he did or not, the phrasing is the same, and the same strict obedience to the slur is necessary.

Generally, phrasing is important in proportion to its being unexpected, e.g. the separation by a slur of the two semiquavers in the theme of the Intermezzo in E minor of Brahms, op. 119 no. 2:

Example 137

See also the first variation of the set he wrote on a theme by Handel: an up-beat of two, not of three semiquavers leads to the second bar, and it is additionally emphasized by the semiquaver rest placed in the lower part of the right hand:

Example 138

here it is essential not to play F″, during the last beat, as just another up-beat-note: its connection with the D″ that precedes it must be heard.

9. Not all problems of accuracy in essentials can be solved. Composers make mistakes;[1] or they change details when the same music reappears later in a piece. Schubert regularly writes something a little differently in his recapitulation sections; and one has to trust that he wanted these slight changes each time, whether they dealt with actual notes, or with dynamics and phrasing. Brahms, in the *da capo* of the B minor Rhapsody, op. 79 no. 1, changes only the last bar of the D minor section; perhaps inadvertently, but the pianist must take the score as he finds it. Just as he cannot make artificial differences where none are written in the score – Schnabel absolutely forbade the playing of a phrase between repeat signs, in a minuet or in a variation, *forte* the first, and *piano* the second time – he cannot edit out any differences of detail which the composer, deliberately or not, left in his score (for instance, the different bass, for no apparent reason, in bars 6 and 7 of Schubert's posthumous Sonata in B flat when these bars return in the recapitulation). Only by playing alike what is alike, and differently what is different, does the performer fulfil the requirements of accurate playing. He may consider these slight differences inessential; but he cannot afford to take the risk of ignoring them and then perhaps discover one day that there was a good reason for the composer to change the music as he did. (See also p. 148.)

(ii) SECONDARY FEATURES

These are markings that the performer may ignore, if he has a good reason, just as he is entitled to suppose the composer himself may occasionally have ignored them. They fall into several categories; here are a few examples.

1. *Repeat signs.* Many of these are essential. The shorter the space

[1] S. Ochs, *Der Deutsche Gesangsverein*, vol. 3, 1926, p. 159, gives a good example from Brahms's *German Requiem*, in which the composer admitted to having written wrong dynamics.

between repeat signs the more important the repeat, as for instance in the theme of Mozart's *Gluck* Variations, K.455. For this reason Schnabel observed the short repeat of the Scherzo of Beethoven's *Spring* Sonata for piano and violin, op. 24, not only the first time, but also during the *da capo* following the Trio. In longer sections, however, the repeat is essential only if it is unusual. The first repeat in an opening or closing movement of classical sonatas can often be omitted, but the second repeat in a sonata movement which has no first repeat (as Beethoven's op. 57, last movement) is striking enough to impose on the performer.

2. *Fingerings* put in by the composer are usually not more than suggestions, but Schnabel insisted that the pianist should at least try them out, for in some instances they point to a special phrasing which might otherwise escape the student; or they affect speed and articulation. At the very end of Brahms's Second Concerto, the composer's fingering, in Schnabel's view, is put there to keep the soloist from getting too fast. Most of Beethoven's fingerings were respected by Schnabel. In some rare cases, however, his editions (also those of Brahms's violin sonatas) recommend a deviation from the fingering suggested by the composer.

3. *Distribution of the hands.* Just as pedal markings, these may be instrumental or musical. If musical, they have to be obeyed; see Schnabel's footnote to the second subject of the Finale of Beethoven's Sonata in D, op. 28. Other examples: Bach, C minor Fantasia, bar 31; Beethoven, Sonata in D minor, op. 31 no. 2, bars 22 ff. Schnabel objected violently to the constant hand-splitting of pianists of the Liszt school;[1] on the contrary he would sometimes play with one hand passages written for two, for the sake of unity of phrasing as at the very beginning of Bach's Chromatic Fantasia; except where the

[1] Two cases of unauthorized hand-splitting which I can remember him using concern the trill at the end of the cadenza for the Finale of Beethoven's Concerto in G, and those written by Brahms in the first movement of the Concerto in D minor, where Schnabel's complex arrangement made them sound more like the orchestral trills.

splitting of hands was intended by the composer to have a rhythmic effect, as in the introduction to Beethoven's Polonaise, op. 89:

Example 139

Here Beethoven makes his intentions doubly clear by writing rests for each hand while the other plays.

Schnabel did not permit, in places where the risks of leaps in the melody part are part of the intended adventure of playing (as in Mozart's Piano Concerto in D, K. 451, first movement, bars 164 and 165), 'cheating' by using two hands. But when the distribution of the two hands was just a matter of pianistic convenience Schnabel had no qualms about changing it. This was especially so when he thought he could achieve better proportions of sound by rearranging the notes of a chord differently between the two hands. In Beethoven's Sonata in C minor, op. 111, he took the upper E flat' of the very opening with his right hand instead of his left, in order to control the sonorities better; and in the opening of Schubert's Sonata in G, op. 78, for the same reason, he played the three lower notes with his left hand, and only the third G'–B' with his right. Immediately afterwards the right thumb took the note B over from the left thumb.

But he never divided a one-hand passage between the hands just for the sake of brilliance, for instance in the E flat arpeggio which occurs 29 bars after the beginning of the solo part in Beethoven's Concerto in C minor, bar 110. There had to be a musical reason to transcend the composer's wishes, even the secondary ones.[1] In other words, the accuracy of the performance always had to be in accordance with the highest possible faithfulness

[1] See his footnote to the octave passage in the coda of the *Waldstein* Sonata Finale.

to the score in sound and in phrasing. It is from this view-point that Schnabel wanted the pianist to make his decision as to how essential any musical detail of the score was for his performance; and in case of doubt he had to observe rather than ignore even the smallest detail noted in the score.

CHAPTER TEN

Interpretation of Character and Structure

Artur Schnabel developed his amazing faculties of concentration to such a degree that they enabled him not only quickly to absorb the spirit of any new piece–often while sight-reading–but also to unearth new secrets about those pieces he knew best. To this effect, he tried first of all to rule out and forget all influences by performances, live and recorded, and all editions other than the original, including his own.[1] The contact with the score was to remain open forever, enabling the musician to continue in his search for additional and ever more profound insight into the music. To my certain knowledge Schnabel rarely listened to his own recordings; he studied each composition afresh, with the result that he often discovered details and connections in it which he had never grasped in perhaps thirty or more years of playing it.

His analysis was, as he said, 'from inside out'. It was concrete inasmuch as he treated each piece as though it were the only composition in existence.[2] I once disputed this and selected the first movement of the *Waldstein* Sonata as my example to ask him: 'How can we understand the originality of the mediant–E major–key for the second subject, unless we know from other sonatas that the new theme "ought" to be presented in the dominant?' His answer was:

---

[1] I once heard him admonish a student who had learned a Beethoven sonata from the Schnabel edition: 'You should at first work with an *Urtext* edition only. Later, you may then compare your results and conceptions with those in my edition.' He often pointed out musical details in lessons which he did not approve of any longer in his edition. His fingerings, however, hardly changed and he affirmed that he continued to practise them every time he relearned these sonatas.

[2] T. W. Adorno uses this term of 'concrete' with the same meaning about Eduard Steuermann's type of analysis, *Diener der Musik*, Tübingen 1965, p. 91.

'The appearance of E major for the second theme would strike us as original, even if we had never known any other sonata movement, for the choice of a remote key is original in itself. If this were not the case, it could not matter to us: mere historic originality, i.e., departure from tradition, concerns the scholar and not the artist.'

In his lessons Schnabel rarely discussed a score or a movement as a whole, preferring to proceed from section to section. As explained in general in Chapter 1, he did not particularly care to check up systematically, in the score in front of him, how Beethoven had developed his motive, Schoenberg had permutated his tone rows, etc. He was interested in the innate drama of the music rather than in the skill of the composer. At all times, he said, the 'what' mattered more to him than the 'how'.[1] Naturally, where in a special case the motivic development affected the very core of the music, Schnabel would call attention to it. Once, while discussing the peaceful serenity of the end of Beethoven's Fourth Piano Concerto, he showed his students how this character is achieved mainly through a simple melodic and harmonic change of the first two bars of the theme:

Example 140

In the *Emperor* Concerto, Schnabel considered the trill which leads into the recapitulation of the Finale as part of the recapitulation

[1] See Konrad Wolff, 'Artur Schnabel', *Piano Quarterly*, no. 84, p. 40.

itself, that is, of the transition section between Adagio proper and the Finale: the B flat originally sustained by the horns now becomes a trill vibration in the solo part, while the soft announcement of the theme is handled this time by the orchestra.[1] Schnabel discovered a similar structure in the Bagatelle in E flat, op. 126 no. 3. In this instance it is even clearer that the replacement of a sustained note in the bass by a trill in the treble is primarily meant as a switch from low to high register. In the *Emperor* Concerto, where this is less obvious, it needs to be brought out by a brilliant top part for the trill.

Except for these and similar passages, Schnabel disregarded motivic developments as such in his search for the inner truth and drama. In Beethoven's Sonata in B flat, op. 22, the development section in the opening movement terminates with a modulatory sequence in which one and the same motive–taken from the end of the exposition–is repeated over and over again: what should interest the performer here is not this motive, but the modulations through various and in part unexpected tonalities for which it serves as vehicle. A similar technique is adopted by Beethoven in his Sonata in A flat, op. 110; during the short development, the first theme is at first played, *crescendo*, over a pedal point on C; from there it proceeds, softly, in sequential modulations of four and four bars (not two and two!) towards the return of the theme in recapitulation. Again, it is not the theme that matters here, but the long line of harmonic-metric structures.[2] As a detail, Schnabel drew the attention of his pupils to the six-four chord of F minor at the end of the *crescendo* phrase which leads directly, without intervening dominant, into the F minor chord proper, played softly: in this combination, the harmony progression and its *crescendo-piano* order is more striking–and therefore more important–than the thematic aspect itself.

The last eight bars of the Prestissimo from the Sonata in E, op. 109, appear to be just another repeat of the terminal phrase:

[1] The rhythmic notation of the theme, this second time, gave Schnabel a clue for the determination of the proper tempo for the transition section, as he specifically stated.

[2] Similar instances can be found in Mozart: e.g. the Adagio in B minor, K.540.

Example 141a

The important event in these bars, however, happens below:[1] beginning in bar 173, the first six bars of the bass motive of the movement are freely quoted in diminution in the left hand.

Example 141b

The E in bar 173 is not only an end, but also the first note of this new phrase. What comes next should be divided into two distinct parts: for three bars the bass, growing in loudness, has the lead. The right-hand harmonies, according to Schnabel, suggest the C major chord of bar 3 of the movement for two-and-a-half bars. In bar 176, the right hand takes over. The left hand, without having finished the diminution of the bass theme, plays a simple *continuo* accompaniment in its last three notes. For this reason, its F sharp in bar 176–already emphasized by octave doubling–remains unaccented. Only the last two bars are played *forte*.

In the context of these pages, what matters is that the apparent motivic structure of this coda turns out to be less important than the complex inferences and evocations suggested by the bass line.

In Schnabel's view the fourth bar (first melody bar) of Schumann's Sonata in G minor is, melodically speaking, an up-beat bar to the next bar whose long melody note makes it heavy.

Example 142a

[1] Schenker's careful analysis of this Sonata, strangely enough, does not mention this.

In order to clarify the up-beat character there must be no break between the first and second beats in the fourth bar. Towards the end of the exposition (bars 83 ff.) the same motive, inverted, appears in the bass and, by the fact of being articulated in the same way, identifies itself subconsciously to the sensitive listener:

Example 142b

Here, however, it becomes the point of departure for a contrapuntal and harmonic display which takes place in all the parts.

Example 142c

The pianist, as Schnabel used to state, must think of many things at once and listen to everything that is going on. He has to avoid any stops in the left hand by, for instance, an interrupting accent on G in bar 1 of Ex. 142 c; he has to combine the duet of the two-part free imitation given to the left hand into one melodious song; but he must not 'underplay' the right hand with its broken-chord harmonies and its fluent rhythmic movement and sweep.[1]

A similar phenomenon may be observed in sets of variation where-ever the unadorned theme is used simultaneously with one of the variations, as in bars 39 ff. of the Adagio of Schubert's *Wanderer* Fantasy: the top notes in the left-hand part are those of the theme while the right hand plays figurations in quick notes round and about these same notes. Schnabel, contradicting the editorial advice of some of the older editions, warned against bringing the left hand out:

[1] About the articulation of these broken chords, see Ex. 203 (p. 165).

'We want to hear the variation now,' he would say.

Beethoven occasionally quotes a motive indistinctly, for instance before the return of the main section in the Scherzo of the *Hammerklavier* Sonata, op. 106, where the notes

Example 143a

mean:

Example 143b

Here Schnabel wanted the rhythm, if not the melody, of the motive made clear as a rhythmic quotation:

Example 143c

See also the E minor section prior to the recapitulation in the Finale of the *Emperor* Concerto:

Example 144a

to be played as:

Example 144b

The coda section of the first movement of Beethoven's last Cello Sonata (D major, op. 102 no. 2) probably also belongs to this category.

Schnabel's unvarying technique of learning and teaching, as he proceeded from section to section in a score, was to consider each note, each phrase, and also each successive section as a challenge to interpretation. 'What happens here?' he constantly asked himself and asked his pupils (though not expecting an answer) as he looked at a new page. His answers, in accordance with the principles developed in the first chapter of this book, were never scientific. They were specific, but untechnical and simple: 'searching for a new key'; 'the rhythmic motion is doubled'; 'the melody now ends on a short note'; 'the texture becomes thicker'; and especially 'nothing new happens here' or, conversely, 'something new is happening, namely . . .' This was necessary to point out if it was not obvious; as in the Finale of Brahms's First Piano Concerto, bar 78, where the music continues without interruption despite the change from semi-quavers to triplet quavers. The opposite situation occurs in the first movement, bar 166 (see Ex. 166 on p. 144).

In other words, what 'happens' refers to what can be heard by any musical layman. Throughout his life, Schnabel, utterly professional though he was, managed to preserve that full direct contact with music as a listener which distinguishes the music-lover, and liked to refer to himself as an 'amateur' in this sense. I shall now try to give a more concrete idea of all this.

In working to understand a score, he always proceeded from the assumption that the composer could have written otherwise but wrote as he did because it was necessary or pleasurable to him. For this reason Schnabel, in explaining a passage, frequently improvised other melodic or harmonic versions which the composer might have selected. He was fascinated by the atypical, as we saw when describing his preoccupation with irregular metrical periods. Daring dissonances appealed to him: the dissonance at the end of the middle section of the slow movement of Mozart's Sonata in C, K.330, for example, and the passing dissonance at the corresponding spot in the second movement of Beethoven's Sonata in F, op. 10 no. 2.

Most music-lovers of Schnabel's generation described the character of a composition in terms of 'happy' or 'sad', 'lyrical' or 'dramatic', etc. Such classification did not appeal to Schnabel himself. He was of the opinion that, in the majority of cases, the sadness or happiness belonged to the listener rather than the piece!

The footnotes and small print in Schnabel's edition of Beethoven's Sonatas indicate some of the more specific 'affects' (to use the historical term) he had discovered in the music. He easily associated this or that section with pairs such as pride or humility, outdoors or indoors, morning or evening, privacy or officialdom, cold or heat, remoteness or directness, agitation or sobriety, etc. Since these associations were largely personal, two illustrations of this will suffice. He conceived the last movement of Schumann's Fantasy, op. 17, as an alternation of descriptive and personal music, the latter beginning at bar 34, and thenceforth alternating with the former in sharply contrasting phases. And he felt that the main theme of the slow movement of Chopin's Sonata in B minor strongly evokes 'morning' when first heard and 'evening' when played again at the end.

The character of a piece can be expressed by the composer at once, or it can develop gradually as the music unfolds. The relative expressive weight of the various sections of a composition was important to Schnabel, and he was sensitive to the over- or understatement given to them. He was irritated for instance when transitions (such as the minor-ninth chords which re-introduce the main section of a number of Schubert Impromptus) were played expressively rather than 'structurally'. There should be no accents, no lingering, and no exaggeration of dynamic nuances in such transitory—and therefore merely functional—bars.

For the rest, Schnabel's concrete analyses dealt mainly with (1) the *inner links* or *connections* which hold a phrase or section together, (2) the *inner separations* inserted by the composer through phrasing and other means, and (3) all the many various *individual* traits occurring in a composition such as the 'hierarchy' of part-writing, the shaping of a main motive, the special 'affects' as they are expressed in strictly musical terms, the contrasts, and similarities, etc.

(i) CONNECTIONS

As for inner connections, we need to distinguish, just as in the field of articulation, between the melodic, harmonic and metric-rhythmic elements.

1. *Melodic connections.* The most important connections are those established by melodic means. The student of a score must invariably discover them and listen to them as he plays since they belong to the essential substance of a work. Schnabel (without, to my knowledge, quoting Schenker) looked at melodic lines as *Urlinien* in basically the same sense in which Schenker used the term. But unlike Schenker he was less preoccupied with the *Urlinie* of the melody in the top part than with the sometimes simpler structural lines of ascent, descent or *ostinato* which are so common in the bass, or in the inner parts. The inner line of the top part melody is not usually of great structural importance, as most melodies depend on an intervallic mobility, made possible precisely by the firmness and consistency of the melody lines in the lower parts.

Very often they take the form of chromatic descents in the bass. A typical example is found in Beethoven's *Waldstein* Sonata. The structure of the opening statement is not determined by the strictly symmetrical melody cast in two rhyming verses of four bars each, but by the steady half-note progression (two bars by two bars) in the bass, from C down to the A below and, from there, with acceleration, to the lowest G:

Example 145

For the performer the concrete value of this bass structure lies in the connection it creates between bar 4 (end of first half of melody) and bar 5 (beginning of second half). All that is necessary is to avoid a *diminuendo* in the left hand at this juncture, in spite of the right-hand phrasing, and to play directly from bar 4 into bar 5.[1]

The same chaconne bass–chromatic descent from key-note to dominant–is frequently found in Chopin and Brahms (e.g. Chopin's Concerto in E minor, first movement, and Waltz in E minor; Brahms's Sonata in F minor, first movement). But other types do occur. Beethoven, in the introduction to his last Sonata, reaches the dominant of C minor in bar 11 by going *up* in the bass. In the coda of Bach's Chromatic Fantasia, a chromatic fall in diminished chords is simultaneously distributed among several parts, including the bottom notes of the top part. The performer, if he focuses on the chords framed by descending minor tenths, can avoid being over-expressive in the top part. Chopin's works, especially the Mazurkas, are full of falling chromatic melodic lines in the inner voices; e.g. the Prelude no. 4 and the Mazurka in A minor, op. 17 no. 4.

As always, wrong accents can make a chromatic melody line unintelligible. In the bass of Schubert's *Wanderer* Fantasy, at the end of the theme, the bass F (bars 14–16) is resolved to E (bar 17). To this effect, the F is brought upward to the higher octave in a chromatic ascending scale in bar 15. By accident, a totally unimportant F sharp–part of this scale–happens to occupy the down-beat of bar 15: if a metrical accent on this note causes an interruption the music 'lacks space to grow in':

Example 146

In Mozart's Piano Concerto in A, K.488, slow movement, bar 20,

---

[1] The same chromatically-descending bass determines the structure of the first six bars of the second movement.

the chromatic descent in the melody begins on F sharp", not E sharp":

Example 147

As for melody lines, even more important than Schenker's *Urlinie* theory is Diran Alexanian's discovery (worked out in his edition of Bach's Cello Suites) of Bach's polyphony hidden within a single part. This occurs also in Mozart, for instance in the third movement of the Concerto in C, K.467, bars 278 ff.

Example 148a

Both the top and the inner notes move melodically. It is important to emphasize the alternation by which one part holds on to a pitch while the other descends. In the first two bars of this example the top notes descend from F" to E"; in the following two, the inner notes descend from C" to B'; etc.

Example 148b

Schnabel admitted that it was difficult to play this clearly yet naturally.

Bass lines frequently move in widely-spaced notes which occasionally fall on off-beats. If so, they should be accented, or else the bass line will not be clear in performance. See Brahms, Sonata in F minor, development section of first movement, bars 4 ff. after the beginning of the D flat major key signature:

Example 149a

Here the bass goes up from D flat to F in three-bar phrases. Each step must be clear to the ear; e.g. E flat, at the beginning of the second phrase, is less important than the initial D flat, since it is only a repeat of a previous E flat in bar 3 of this example:

Example 149b

See also the bass line that descends chromatically from F sharp to E in the section of Bach's Chromatic Fantasia immediately preceding the coda. The structural accent necessary in all such passages can be given quite strongly without danger of interference with the melody line, because of an astonishing capacity of the human brain for remembering the sound of one note vigorously struck until the next similar note comes along, quite undisturbed by any notes which may have been sounded in the meantime.

When several parts of the music, particularly bass and treble, collaborate to create a chromatic or diatonic melody line which holds the score together, Schnabel would re-enforce its audibility by deliberately confronting any notes that succeed one another in the extreme registers, e.g. Mozart, Piano Concerto in A, K.488, Cadenza of first movement, bars 15–19:

Example 150

Schnabel accented the two top notes in the right hand so that they would be heard as up-beats to the down-beat notes of the left. Playing of the right-hand arpeggios in almost strict time helped him to reach this goal.

The same principles apply to *pedal points* and other held or repeated notes during changing harmonies, especially in the bass.[1] The pedal point is not always obvious, as in the coda of Brahms's

[1] Schnabel's definition of pedal point included its description as a quiescent harmonic center. A "genuine pedal point" he called any sustained note above which there are harmony progressions exceeding simple changes of tonic and dominant.

Rhapsody in B minor, op. 79 no. 1.[1] Here the pianist must give it sufficient emphasis to establish it as the main connecting event in this final section. For repeated bass notes in a higher register, the same rule is even more important, as, for example, in Mozart's last Piano Concerto, K.595, Finale, bar 65:

Example 151

The accents given to each of the four B flats must be independent and equal. In bar 4 of this example, the B flat in the left hand must be considerably louder than the middle C' equally played by the left hand. The *ostinato* bass is the 'connecting tissue' without which the shape of the phrase would be lost.

The *ostinato* can switch from one part to another, as in the last variation of Beethoven's Sonata in E, op. 109, where the dominant note B, presented first in repeated notes, then in measured trills, and finally in quick trills alternating between the extreme registers of the instrument, lasts throughout the entire variation.

Ostinato ideas in the top part follow the same rules. In bars 22–25 of the slow movement of Schubert's *Wanderer* Fantasy each phrase ends on the dominant note and chord at the end of the bar:

Example 152

Schnabel got his pupils to play these four final chords with a veritable *sforzàto* in both hands in order to bring out the excitement and suspense of these repeated notes and chords. In his Sonata in A minor, op. 42, Schubert uses a similar technique of composing for the first twenty-five bars: the terminal melody note E is to be

[1] See p. 35.

underlined at each repeat by phrasings rather than accents in order to bring out the introductory character of these bars.

2. *Harmonic connections.* These are usually simpler to spot, because the most obvious harmonic events are, as a rule, those which the performer must concentrate on, such as modulations to a closely-related key, a return to a previous key, etc. The harmonic connections between the different movements of a sonata or suite, from Bach and Mozart to Beethoven, Schubert and the Romantics, can sometimes be an important element in the unifying process. The brushes with C sharp minor in the opening movement of Schubert's posthumous Sonata in B flat must challenge the pianist to evoke the spectre of the slow movement, written in this key, for a moment. The E minor passage in Beethoven's Fourth Piano Concerto, first movement, bars 102ff., absolutely must be played as a mirage-like anticipation of the atmosphere of the second movement. Here we can see that what really makes for individual harmony is not anything discernible in ordinary analysis, but rather the precise vertical arrangement of its notes; in this case, the wide spacing of the minor chord with the third on top. As another example, compare the writing of the C sharp minor harmonies in the outer movements of Beethoven's Sonata in C sharp minor, op. 27 no. 2:

Example 153a

Example 153b

Extended modulations often hold an entire section together on their own. The musician, if he happens to be unfamiliar with a particular piece by Haydn, Mozart or Beethoven, still knows very well which key a certain modulation must eventually lead him to, even if it is going astray for a while, and can thus perceive the road taken by the composer—straight, curved, back and forth, or whatever its direction may be—with pleasurable suspense, until the preordained goal is attained. If he wants to hold his performance together in such passages, the performer must share this feeling of inherent musical drama and suspense. In the recapitulation of the *Waldstein* Sonata, op. 53, by Beethoven, the second subject appears at first in A major, which is the key 'below' E major (in which the theme was presented in the exposition). But it is clear that eventually the main key of C major will have to be reached again. The modulation which accomplishes this change of key during the second half of the theme (bars 5–8) is therefore a major structural event. This becomes clear according to Schnabel, if the theme here is more simply—that is, less expressively—presented; somewhat in the style of an improvised modulation on the organ, with the D minor chord at the end of bar 6 of the subject being 'the most important'.

Sequences were used by Schnabel wherever possible to secure the long line of the music. The structure of extended sequences cannot be neglected without damage to the architectural presentation of the music. Where the same melodic figurations are to be played four times in succession, each two of these usually belong together and form a superior unit. In the coda of the Finale of Schumann's Piano Concerto, the figure

Example 154a

occurs four times, introduced each time by a *sforzato* chord. By playing the second and fourth of these *sforzato* chords as resolutions of the first and third, and therefore more softly, Schnabel conveyed the harmonic complexity of the sequence better than if he had played them all alike, and he secured the long line of the sweeping music as it leads to the climactic end:

Example 154b

In order to find the structurally important harmonic progressions, it is necessary to forget everything else. One good method is to play the harmonic rhythms in simple chords, like a continuo accompaniment. Schnabel often used this method in lessons to clarify the harmonic structure. In the Finale of Schubert's Sonata in A minor, op. 42, for instance, the same phrase, with variants, is presented twice in succession, between bars 108 and 123. But the first time (bar 108 to the down-beat of bar 115) the music modulates from A minor to E minor—hence Schubert's *crescendo*—while the second time (bar 115, second beat to bar 123, down-beat) the new key is simply confirmed—hence no further *crescendo*. Despite the melodic and metric correspondence, the interpreter of this music must observe these differences above all.

3. *Rhythmic-metric connections* (or what in laymen's language is usually referred to as 'the rhythm of the piece'). A good example for the unifying function of rhythms is provided by Beethoven's Seventh Symphony in which, with the exception of the Scherzo, every movement opens with a three-note rhythm in which the first note is longer than the two others. Each of these dactylic rhythms is presented at first exclusively on the dominant note E. Such unifying devices serve much the same purpose as verse metre in a poem—although in music there is infinitely more verse variety possible than in poetry.

In some works the rhythm of the piece is its main motive; in some, it is just a pulse or vibration or whatever one wants to call it;

and in others it is both: for instance, in the Violin Concerto by Beethoven. Here the four drum beats of the first bar are the pulse as well as the main motive. In the first bar of his Piano Sonata in D, op. 28, though externally similar, the bass notes played in the first bar are only pulse, not thematic material. On the contrary, the opening of the Finale of the Sonata in E flat, op. 31 no. 3, is rhythmic motive, but not pulse.

Rhythmic events become important in particular whenever the melody pitch is unvarying, because the listeners' attention then shifts automatically to the time element. Schubert's music receives its rhythmic character largely through this device; e.g. the repeated notes of the melody in the beginning of the *Wanderer* Fantasy; the Impromptu in B flat, op. 142 no. 3; the Sonata in A, op. 120, first movement, second subject; and the second and fourth bars of the F minor *Moment Musical*, op. 94 no. 3. Wherever these repeated notes had to be played, Schnabel very carefully insisted on their correct articulation: equally long, fully detached—that is each note produced by individual physical impulse—and with minimal (if any) metrical accent on down-beats. Thus one is enabled to feel the tensile strength of this delicate rhythm on which the whole structure reposes. Whenever the rhythm consists of a crotchet followed by two quavers, as in many of the examples quoted, it is the second quaver that needs special attention so that it emerges not as an underprivileged partner—too early and too soft—after its two more conspicuous companion-notes.

Another unifying rhythmic device frequently to be found in Schubert is the accented second beat in the bass of a composition in ¾ time. The classic example is the Impromptu in E flat, op. 90 no. 2, in which this bass rhythm unifies the main section and the Trio.

Both these devices combine in one of the most ingratiating passages of his piano music, in the Scherzo of his Sonata in D, op. 53:

Example 155a

In the odd bars of this example, each of the three beats contains an accent marked by the composer! What happens in reality is a rhythmic counterpoint, as it were, between two typical Schubert rhythms: in the right hand the even-note rhythm, as in bars 2 and 4 of the F minor *Moment Musical* op. 94 no. 3; in the left hand, the accented second-beat rhythm, as in the Impromptu in E flat. Schnabel made this charming combination clear by not allowing any of the right-hand accents to be shared by the left hand, and also by phrasing from the second beat of each bar to the down-beat of the next:

Example 155b

To this effect he landed possibly a trifle late on each second beat, and very much in time on each down-beat in the left hand. Towards the end of the phrase, he allowed a little extra time for the G minor chord, embedded as it is between two B flat major chords. But by understating Schubert's accents and by keeping the *rubato* to an absolute minimum, Schnabel not only prevented this waltz-like passage from sounding vulgarly 'Viennese', but he also secured its floating quality.

In Schubert's innumerable 'oom-pah' accompaniments, the '-pah' always has a syncopating effect, as though it were played by another instrument.[1] This rhythmic device is an important element in Schubert's personal musical language. Schnabel used to speak of 'three-hand music' here, because the only easy way to achieve the correct articulation for these accompaniments is to play them in both hands–which he then recommended doing as a practice method, in order to train the ear control prior to practising accompaniment and melody together.

Chopin's rhythmic devices are sometimes polyrhythmic, e.g. the Etude in F minor, op. 25 no. 2, and the Waltz in A flat, op. 42. They have to be presented clearly and independently, just as in Beethoven.[2] The difference is that, what in Beethoven is just 'by-play', here becomes a thematic element.

[1] See Ex. 57, p. 57 above.   [2] See Ex. 110 ff., p. 98 above.

Brahms's famous so-called syncopated rhythms, on the other hand, for the most part have a diversifying rather than unifying effect. The Capriccio in D minor, op. 116 no. 7, is an exception:

Example 156a

Here the long-short in each hand alternates with that of the other. It is played *diminuendo* in the right hand, and *crescendo* in the left. The fingering imposed by Brahms makes this possible. In other words, in both hands the second beat is the softer one. Schnabel demonstrated this in a simplification which he played approximately as follows:

Example 156b

Heard in this way, the music easily flows from bar to bar, and the rhythmic device is unifying inasmuch as it brings the long melody line out, as Schnabel wanted it, because the danger of 'chopped-up' performances–bar by bar–is especially great here.

In *dances* and dance-like compositions the basic rhythm is, of course, the most obvious necessity in performance.[1] Schnabel always explained any essential dance rhythm in great detail. This included Bach's suites and partitas. Unfortunately, my notes and recollections of lessons on these are incomplete. I only remember

---

[1] It seems superfluous to add that rhythm is carried by the bottom parts, and therefore hard to understand why F. E. Kirby, *A Short History of Keyboard Music* (1966) p. 136, tries to identify sarabande rhythms by their *top* parts.

that in sarabandes he insisted that the third bar of each four-bar phrase should be presented with all three beats being part of the rhythm—in contrast to the first, second, and fourth bars in which only the first two beats belong to it. He saw *Allemandes* as "pleasant, round, and fully transparent" dances moving in quavers as their time units. In *Courantes* of the type used in most English Suites and Partitas, the alternation of $\frac{3}{2}$ and $\frac{6}{4}$ must be clearly evident; and he recommended, to this effect, separating the two halves of each bar in both metres, by means of starting a new phrase on the fourth crotchet.

In a lesson on Debussy's *La Puerta del Viño* Schnabel taught the *habanera* rhythm as a dotted rhythm in which it is necessary to accent the semiquaver following the dot. He explained the *mazurka* rhythm as one in which the third beat is accented in alternate bars—not in every bar. In general, he described a mazurka as a 'dance in which the music goes round and round'. See Chopin's Mazurka in A minor, op. 68 no. 2:

Example 157

In a *waltz* rhythm, though much latitude is needed in order to deal with the very different kinds of waltzes, the one common element is that the third beat is always lighter than the first two which, together, form the heavy beat, in a limping two-beat bar, as it were. This requirement is so basic that Schnabel insisted on its fulfilment in other pieces than waltzes, if they had the same rhythmic configuration. The third beat had to be softer than the second, for instance, in the theme of Chopin's Ballade in G minor; in that of Mozart's Rondo in A minor, K.511; and in the first variation of the theme of the Finale of Beethoven's Sonata in E, op. 109: all three are very serious pieces in which nobody ought to think of a waltz, but should respect the waltz aspect of the rhythm.

Many Schumann pieces have a walking rhythm which has to be treated as yet another dance rhythm, as for instance in 'Glückes genug' from his *Kinderszenen*. At the end of this piece, the continued steps must be secured despite the slowing-down marked by the composer. Schnabel's way of protecting the basic rhythm was that he made no *ritardando* in the semiquavers preceding each step. He played them at the same absolute speed as before in spite of the slowed-down pulse, and thus, in the listener's mind, their identity was preserved.

Finally, since sharp rhythms are divisive rather than unifying in their effect, it seemed occasionally opportune to Schnabel, in order to hold a long phrase together, to add up the different rhythms of the various parts and combine them. In bar 17 of the slow movement of Beethoven's *Waldstein* Sonata, he thought, for instance, in terms of five continuous demisemiquavers (rather than in terms of two in the treble plus three in the bass) at the end of the bar:

Example 158a   Example 158b

(See also Ex. 78, above.)

(ii) SEPARATIONS
(*especially through phrasing*)

In connecting some parts in an organic whole we automatically disconnect others, and vice versa. At each juncture our attention is directed to what is not already 'taken care of' by the composer. When something new begins something old is continuing all the same. This is the first clue to the idea of phrasing. Phrasing can be thought of as a separation, and yet there is much more to it. The last note of one phrase is frequently the first note of the next. The second half of one phrase can become the first half of the next. An entire phrase can retroactively be heard as the first part of another phrase. Many instances are ambiguous, as for example the middle section of Schumann's *Kreisleriana*, no. 5:

Example 159a

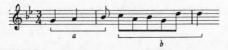

It is impossible to reconcile the initial order of the two segments of this melody with the end of the section where their order is reversed.

Example 159b

Schumann probably meant the phrase to be heard in both ways. Therefore the pianist must avoid separating the two halves too much. Many subtleties of phrasing are just for the pianist-performer alone. This is most important in quick passages: their phrasing 'is not supposed to be more than the interpreter's private amusement and can be observed by the listener only as a means of making figurations sound pleasant rather than mechanical'. Schnabel gave suggestions of this kind on the fast middle section of Chopin's Ballade in A flat and in the Finale of his Sonata in B minor, because sub-dividing is a psychological necessity here: in both cases, he recommended his pupils to think of the continuous semiquaver runs as being phrased from the fourth semiquaver of one bar to the third in the next; but so subtly that it would not have an interrupting effect.

Example 160

Example 161

In some cases, such as the first bar of Beethoven's Fourth Piano Concerto, it was important to Schnabel to suggest more than one phrasing. Beginning at the down-beat, he recommended starting a new (sub-) phrase on each of the four quavers in turn, that is:

Example 162

Quite often, especially in older music, two apparently contrasting melodic elements within one section or even within one phrase are in reality merely different realizations of the same material. Schnabel explained this at the beginning of Schubert's Impromptu in A flat, op. 90 no. 4. The broken chords in the first four bars are basically identical with the unbroken ones in the next two bars. They relate to each other like water to ice; and one could imagine Schubert arranging them conversely as follows:

Example 163

However, if the composer wants to blur the start of a new section, or, sometimes, even the entry of the opening theme by sneaking it in, as it were, it would be very wrong for the interpreter to split what the composer wanted to join simply because the formal outline tells him to do so. There are many examples in which Schnabel simply acknowledged the absence of a separation and did not try to add one of his own. To this category belongs, for instance, the bar preceding the left-hand presentation of the rondo theme in Beethoven's Sonata in B flat, op. 22:

Example 164a

The entire bar becomes an up-beat to this entry, and it is not permissible to isolate the last three or the last six of these semiquavers from the others and make them into the alleged rebeginning of the theme.

Example 164b

(A very similar situation occurs at the corresponding spot in the Finale of Beethoven's op. 24, the *Spring* Sonata for piano and violin in F major.) The beginnings of Chopin's Second and Fourth Ballades are similarly constructed. Quite obviously, the composer intended to veil the opening of the first theme by using repeated notes as an introduction; and just as obviously the pianist must not frustrate this intention by waiting at one point or another, or by accenting this or that note.[1] Finally, one must mention here the entry of the *Arioso dolente* from Beethoven's Sonata in A flat, op. 110: the preparatory chords must not stop at all, but continue uninterruptedly as the song begins.

With irregular phrase-lengths, phrasing can become a big problem. In bars 369–76 of the Finale of Schubert's Sonata in G, op. 78, Schnabel at one time suggested as marked here on top:

Example 165

Later, he made a different suggestion (see bottom of Ex. 165). Each of these divisions illuminates different aspects of the structure.

[1] I heard Schnabel illustrate the nature of the opening of the Fourth Ballade by playing a much greater number of the initial octave G's before continuing (uninterruptedly, of course) with what follows.

As for the means of phrasing, just as we avoid accents where we want no interruption, we make them, especially on off-beat notes, where an interruption is desired, i.e. where we wish to begin a new phrase. If necessary we make an accent as well as wait for a moment, as in bar 166 of Brahms's Piano Concerto in D minor, after the first quaver:

Example 166

Otherwise the danger of the two melodies running into each other like an ink blot is too great. The accent of interruption, however, has to be softer than the expressive accent on F″ which follows.

These examples cannot give even an approximate guide to phrasing. Phrasing, in its minute shadings, is perhaps the most individual part of a performance; and Schnabel's solutions in many instances were personal to him, as attentive listeners to his recordings have found out.

(iii) CLARIFICATION OF INDIVIDUAL FEATURES IN EACH WORK

The 'identity' of each composition, and of each section within a composition, is what concerns us here; i.e. whatever it is that makes us recognize *this* piece of music as different from all others; *this* section, as different from the section just heard. The infinite combinations of *contrast* and *continuity* in art have occupied our attention earlier in this book; their contemplation is one of the main points of departure which will serve us now in the task of identifying a composition and its parts for the purposes of performance. When the thematic material of the exposition returns in the recapitulation, for instance, it must be played the same—for instance, the phrasings must remain similar enough to permit identification—but it must also reflect the development of the piece as a whole which took place in between. Schnabel liked to point to any details that change during the course of a piece. In the Scherzo of the *Hammerklavier* Sonata, Beethoven marks the very beginning with a *crescendo* from the up-beat to the down-beat. In bar 14 the same notes are marked *diminuendo*. In Schubert's A-flat Impromptu, op. 142 no. 2, in which the final phrase (bars 31–38) is partly repeated (bars 35–42), a crescendo leads from the sixth to the seventh measure at first; but when the phrase is repeated this crescendo appears one bar earlier.

He was sensitive to differentiations of long and short notes, especially long and short endings, within one phrase. According to his interpretation, the three repeated notes A′ in bar 2 of Mozart's last Sonata in D, K.576, must be played (as he would sing it): 'short–and–long'.

Example 167

The first A′ still belongs to the–*non-legato*–opening bar, while the other two A's form a bridge towards the next bar.

When the introductory note of Schubert's Impromptu in C minor, op. 90 no. 1, twice reappears during the coda (bars 194 ff.)

Example 168a

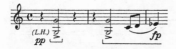

it is followed by a rest only the first time; the second time it goes directly into what follows; and the same differentiation occurs four bars later when the parts are reversed.

Example 168b

Similar notation exists in the coda of the opening movement of Schubert's posthumous Sonata in B flat, bar 341:

Example 169

In both compositions Schnabel considered the difference between isolated and held notes to be very important for the pianist.

At the opening of Beethoven's Sonata in E minor, op. 90, bar 2 and its up-beat consist of quavers followed by rests; bar 3f. and their up-beats have crotchets. Beethoven wrote a deliberately imperfect echo here which was important to Schnabel.

Example 170

He had an ear for 'rhymes' and believed that their clarification was necessary for the presentation of melodies. The ascending melodic arpeggio in bar 57 of the Finale of Schubert's Sonata in G finds its counterpart in the descending one, two bars later.

Example 171

Both times Schubert marked the end note of the arpeggio with an accent. This means, of course, that there must be no right-hand accent on the down-beats of these two bars.

In the fugato subject of the fifth variation in Beethoven's Sonata in E, op. 109,

Example 172

the last two notes (descending major thirds) present a diminution of the first two. This important melodic relationship is usually ignored in performance because the pianist, when he plays the second bar, is too busy in presenting the imitation which begins there. But in the variation theme itself the two pairs of thirds were written to be played at the same speed, so that the new melodic element of variation 5 is precisely this diminution. To make it audible, the B at the end of the second bar must be as loud as the D sharp preceding.

The first number in Schumann's *Kinderszenen* ('Von fremden Ländern und Menschen') has identical melody notes (B′ and G″) in bars 1, 3 and 5.

Example 173

But the music of bar 5 is different from the others owing to the insertion of the long note G in the left hand. In order to clarify this difference in performance, Schnabel suggested starting bars 1 and 3 with a melody accent followed by a *diminuendo* in ascending to the second note; but starting bar 5 softly in the right hand and reaching the high note this time by making a *crescendo*.

At the end of the first section of Brahms's Rhapsody in B minor, op. 79 no. 1 (bars 22 ff.), a sustained theme is played twice, the second time at half speed, with the end figure repeated (as Schubert does at the end of the first movement of his *Divertissement à la Hongroise*):

Example 174a

Schnabel saw to it that this structural broadening of the music at the end of the main exposition was clarified by accenting the fourth and last F sharp′, at the end of bar 25 (and to which the composer's *crescendo* mark leads up), as though the music had been written as:

Example 174b

(cf. Ex. 103 p. 94).

But it must be repeated that, if all differences ought to be observed in performance, when there is *no* difference it is wrong artificially to create one. Schnabel was violently upset by externally imposed echo effect, soft repeats of a section played loudly the first time, and other such violations of taste, which have been discussed earlier. He gave his pupils the warning example of Bruno Walter, whom he loved and respected, but who had played the second subject of Mozart's Concerto in A, K.488, first movement, slower and *rubato* in the first half, though resuming the full tempo and simple expression when he conducted the second half, which is played by the orchestra. To Schnabel, the urge to play unequally what was conceived as equal revealed a lack of sense of structure.

In bar 142 of Brahms's First Piano Concerto *all* the top notes are melody notes:

Example 175a

in order to establish a variant from the clarinet parts in bar 46:

Example 175b

In his Second Piano Concerto in B flat the soloist enters in the second bar. The E flat''' on the fourth beat of this measure must not carry any interrupting melody accent and be played strictly as an unemphasized up-beat, as was mentioned earlier.

Example 176

Unlike the statement of the motive by the French horn, this echo is part of a continuous triplet-motion which begins precisely with the triplet played by the horn. The piano picks up this rhythm and perpetuates it. Schnabel's interpretation was in time, 'light, dreamy'; so that it was possible to listen to the constant B flat major harmony in this solo without disturbance.

Variation 7 of Brahms's *Handel* Variations has repeated notes in the right hand topping the melodic variant of the theme. The trumpet-like tone colour of the repeated notes makes them more important than the theme below—which can be heard clearly in any case. Therefore the pianist has to focus on the top part:

Example 177

There are similar cases in the last section of the B minor Capriccio, op. 76 no. 2

Example 178

and Beethoven, Sonata in F, op. 10 no. 2, Finale, bar 69, where the repeated note is prepared by an exciting measured trill on A″ with its lower semitone in the preceding bar:

Example 179

This trill is an example of quick motion enlivening the spirit and sweep of a piece—it may also be a tragic one—which, as a movement, has to be brought out, even if it happens to be confined to the accompaniment. Three examples:

Schumann, Sonata in G minor, first movement, coda:

Example 180

Beethoven, *Pathétique* Sonata, first movement:

Example 181

Cf. also Brahms, Sonata in F minor, Finale, first episode.

In all three pieces Schnabel insisted on making the inner voices vibrate intensely.

When a melody, in the manner of a vocal duet, moves in parallel thirds, sixths, or tenths, the lower part, though played less loudly for acoustic reasons[1] must be heard as 'co-leading', as it were. This

[1] See p. 162.

applies, for instance, to the theme of the slow movement of Beethoven's Sonata in A, op. 2 no. 2: from the opening chord, in which the top notes of each hand introduce the first note of the theme, both parts must be heard in their 'togetherness'. [1]

The basic harmonic rhythm of a varied theme is to be maintained in the variations, i.e. in Mozart's Concerto in B flat, K.450, second movement, the *crescendo* to the second beat in bar 2.

Example 182

As for the *character* of a composition, the principal error of interpreters is, on the whole, to lose its proportions, and therefore the balance, during performance by over-concentrating on one aspect at the expense of all the others, or to confine certain expressions to one chord, or one bar, when in reality they ought to be distributed over an entire phrase or episode in the piece. This was pointed out to pupils in connection with many of the *sforzato* markings by Beethoven, *ritardando* markings by Schumann, etc. They must be interpreted in the light of the expression needed for the phrase or episode as a whole.

Schnabel spoke of the *general character* of a work but rarely, and then to point out the particular *tensions* inherent in the music. In the First Prelude of Book I of the *Well-Tempered Clavier*, the harmonic tension resolves itself as soon as the bass arrives at the note G in bar 24. [2] In the middle section of the second movement of Schubert's posthumous Sonata in B flat, a mystic state of expectancy stops everything for a second before the bass moves down from F to E (bar 67); Schnabel said to wait here until one was inwardly ready to experience this resolution in stillness:

[1]See also Sonata op. 28, I, second theme.
[2]But Schnabel would not tolerate a *ritardando* in bar 23 as the generation before him had done!

Example 183

To end with, I should like to include some of the remarks Schnabel once made during a single lesson concerning the structure and character of the exposition of the opening movement of Beethoven's Sonata in D, op. 10 no. 3, pointing to 'what happens here' at each step.

1. The initial heavy up-beat leads *legatissimo* into the down-beat. This identifies the motive and must be observed throughout the entire movement. It recurs in the Finale.

2. The first phrase ends with bar 16, not bar 10. Bar 16 is to be played *fortissimo*.

3. Bars 23–38. Every four beats constructed as H–H–L–L.[1]

4. Bars 38–45. Intensity increasing. After bar 40 'precipitation from all sides'. Pedal through the whole of bar 45. In this bar the first note–A″–is important, because it is not resolved into G sharp until the beginning of bar 47, two bars later.

5. The second subject is a triptych, part 1 and part 3 ending on G sharp′–E′:

Example 184

No rush in bars 56–60, and no accent on A′ on the third beat of bar 58. The G sharp″ in bar 65 echoes that of bar 63.

6. Bars 71–74: the melodic interval of an ascending semitone (C sharp to D) is played four times by the right hand. The subsequent *crescendo* should be achieved by emphasizing the various dominant

---

[1] See Ex. 67, p. 64.

notes for which Beethoven's *sforzato* marks are meant. Some of them are single; some enforced by octave doublings.

7. In bars 86 ff., the top part is phrased through the ascending intervals:

Example 185

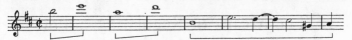

8. Bars 93–113. Re-affirmation of final cadence by means of repeated ascending A major scales (93–97; 98–101; 102–5), beginning with the lowest A in bar 93, as a melodic connection in the sense explained earlier in this chapter.

9. In bar 113 the bass–*ostinato* on A–initiates a new metrical unit. The phrasing here has to submit to the bass structure and must not be subservient to the conflicting melody patterns which begin three beats later, also in the left hand, and are echoed by the right hand.[1]

Example 186

These right-hand figurations, being just space-filling doodlings, as it were, were marked *pianissimo* by the composer. To understand this section, it is helpful to read and play at first the left-hand part alone, as all the essentials are concentrated in it.

[1] Paul Fontaine, *Basic Formal Structures in Music*, New York 1967, p. 135, not only ignores the importance of the bass for the determination of metrical periods, but also prints the bass wrongly in his example so that the ties between the bass notes fit the melodic pattern instead of–as Beethoven had it–contradicting it.

CHAPTER ELEVEN

The Means of Regulating Sound

TONE COLOUR

Artur Schnabel studied the tone colour of piano sound not as a scientist, but as an artist. It fascinated him that, although piano tone colour is quite distinctive, it remains the same throughout the entire range of the instrument, whereas a clarinet, for instance, playing its lowest notes, sounds like a different instrument from the sound of its high register. He often said that Beethoven was fully aware of this, and that he exploited this fact from his early days (as in Var. 15 of *Eroica* Variations, bars 22–30) in the many passages where very high and very low notes form a musical unit in which they disappear as distinct individual parts. No orchestration of Beethoven's piano sonatas—using double-bass versus piccolo, or other such combinations—can achieve this homogeneity of sound, enabling the listener to focus on the harmony and voice-leading.

Perhaps because of this acoustic phenomenon (which Schnabel did not attempt to define in scientific terms), piano tone has—as Schnabel expressed it—a quality of *neutrality*.[1] By this, he simply meant to describe the fact that, listening to a piano, it is easy to imagine all sorts of various instruments playing this music. For instance, I play a symphony I have never heard on the piano from a piano duet score: the orchestral sound is automatically present by association. The other keyboard instruments, especially the harpsichord and the organ, cannot lend themselves to the same purpose. Their special timbre is incompatible with that of other instruments in the listener's mind, because it intrudes too much on their perception as a tone colour of its own.

[1] Artur Schnabel, *My Life and Music*, ed. E. Crankshaw, 1961, p. 178.

This brings up the practical question whether the pianist is entitled or, in some cases, perhaps also compelled to strive for the imitation of the sound of other instruments; whether he should, for instance, play certain themes trying to sound like an oboe; certain others, imitating a violin, etc. It was obvious to Schnabel that, in some works, this has to be done. When, in bars 80 and 82 of the slow movement of the Piano Concerto in A, K.488, Mozart let the pianist share the accompaniment with the second bassoon

Example 187

he intended it to sound homogeneous, and Schnabel therefore asked his pupils to imitate the even, *non-legato* sound produced by the bassoon as closely as possible. There are many examples in Mozart's works, including some of the solo sonatas and fantasias–in which the piano is similarly treated, that is, as another wind instrument. But occasionally Mozart attempts still more. Schnabel treated passages throughout the entire A major Sonata, K.331, and not only the Finale *alla turca*, as Turkish music, and pointed out that the octave passages in the third variation, the cross-hand figurations in the fourth (and in the Trio section of the Minuet) and, of course, the final variation are supposed to suggest the various sound effects which Mozart produces in the orchestration of his *Entführung*. The Sonata, in Schnabel's conception of it, was a *tour de force*, presumably written for the composer's own use, in which he could show his ability to transport the audience to Turkey on a magic carpet of sonorities.

Nevertheless, these cases are exceptional and Schnabel insisted that, in the great majority of compositions, their authors, when they wrote for piano, wanted their music to sound like piano music and nothing else.[1] Schnabel agreed with Beethoven, Mendelssohn,

[1] It was his conviction that in the act of composing, a composer normally first invents the music itself and only then thinks of its possible orchestration.

Schumann, Brahms, etc. that Bach's music, too, should be played as music for the piano whenever it is played on this instrument. He believed that one ought to play Bach on the piano with all the sonorities of which the piano of today is capable, in order to bring out the structure, articulation, and character of the music in a natural manner. In the same connection he once said, 'Can you imagine Beethoven in his late years refusing to play one of his early piano sonatas on the grounds that his present instrument sounded entirely different?'

Even when playing transcriptions (Liszt's arrangement of Paganini *Etudes*, etc.) he deemed it a mistake to try and imitate the tone colour of the original instrument. Transcriptions are of value in their own right, and the performer should be concerned with showing how the music has retained its own identity in its new dress.

True, our feeling for sound effects is enriched by orchestral or instrumental associations. Occasionally outright imitation is permissible and desirable. In the much abused piano part of the 'Serenade' from Schubert's *Schwanengesang* the piano is clearly meant to imitate a lute. Schnabel did not use any pedal in this song.

In certain of Weber's works too it is scarcely possible to avoid the orchestral sound associations suggested by the music. The first movement of his D minor Sonata is built so that it seems possible to distinguish between symphonic and piano parts. In the *Invitation to the Dance* one hears groups of wind instruments and groups of strings. But the charm of the association lies in the pianistic reproduction of these tone colours, which is why Berlioz's orchestral arrangement of the *Invitation to the Dance* never satisfies the ear.

The works of certain French composers, particularly Debussy, often tempt the pianist to concentrate solely on the tone colour, to the neglect of other important elements of the music. It goes without saying that sound plays a major role in all Debussy's works, but they are first and foremost music with all that it denotes: form, harmonic structure, melodic line, rhythmical framework. These elements, here as everywhere else, are what matters most to the interpreter. The piano is colourful only through articulation of one kind or another. The more deeply the instrument penetrates into the phrasing, the internal rhythms, the harmonic successions of a composition, the more richly will the pianist be able to colour it, whereas the vague and indeterminate sound masses that used to be the stock-in-trade for Debussy-players only serve to make all of his compositions sound alike. To obtain his characteristic colouring it is sometimes necessary to be very peremptory, and almost aggressive.

The pianist need not always use the brightest colours, but even when he restricts himself, as it were, to neutral black and white tones, he must be sure they are etched clearly and beautifully. If he uses many colours, their scintillations, like those of a prism, must unite to form a whole. Changes in tone colour are closely connected with the alternation of objective and subjective music. The relative importance of harmony and melody in a piece of music also influences the sound. When the harmonic element prevails, the tones are less sharply separated, and the colours run.

Obviously, with the exception of the soft pedal, the piano has no means of altering its timbre. Colouring must almost always be accomplished by indirect means. Shading of tone-intensity is one of the most valuable tools with which a pianist can work. Shading depends not only on the manner in which the key is struck, but among other things also on the manner of its release. If it is released quickly, the retroactive intensity is likely to be increased. It is a mistake to imagine that all notes should be played with equal intensity or even be clearly audible. In order to clarify the *music* it is often necessary to make certain *notes* obscure.[1]

The pedal can and should be of assistance. The simultaneous vibration of all the notes—not the mere holding down of those already struck—alters the timbre. In the development section of the first movement of his Sonata, op. 79, bar 67, Beethoven prescribed the pedal with a view towards colouring. This is a suitable passage for studying the indirect tone colours of the piano. The same music just previously played (bars 59–65), now sounds as though coming from a different instrument. There are a number of reasons for this: (1) the tonality is changed, (2) the dynamics are different (*p dolce* instead of *f*), (3) the *sforzato* on the second left-hand crotchet is

[1] To avoid misunderstanding it must be pointed out that intensity of tone is not identical with pressure of physical touch.

omitted, (4) the left hand now plays *non-legato* rather than *staccato*, and most of all (5) the pedal is held down.

Example 188a   Example 188b

(senza Ped.)

Ped.

It is not always right to use pedal in *quasi-tremolo* passages, as is usually done. They often sound more genuine when played *legatissimo* without pedal.[1] One can assume that this is the intention of many composers, such as Schubert, in the beginning of his C Major Fantasia for Violin and Piano (cf. p. 103).

When pedal is designated (especially in Beethoven) for a passage covering several harmonies, the contours of the notes must be articulate yet softly rounded, so that they merge into a common colouring. A full, soft sound in the middle registers is important here. The problem of colouring can be studied in the beginning of the last movement of the *Waldstein* if only these harmonies are played:

Example 189

(The tonic harmony is the more important. It is not extinguished by the dominant.)

Decisive for the tone colour of the second subject in the Finale of Beethoven's Fourth Piano Concerto are the descending notes in the left hand, bars 6–8 of the example:

[1] Schnabel managed to achieve this effect in bars 14 ff. of the *Waldstein* Sonata.

Example 190

Unlike other elements of performance, tone colour depends largely on acoustic conditions. It is therefore a mistake for teachers, students and other performers to plan the exact pedalling for each piece ahead of time. There must be flexibility left to cope spontaneously with an unexpected acoustic situation, created by the hall, or the piano, or both. This is why Schnabel objected to educational editions prescribing the pedal to be used in every bar once and for all. Most pianists cannot say exactly how they used the 'instrumental' pedal, and, according to Schnabel, this is as it should be. Of course, pedal may not be used to cover up momentary technical slips and imperfections of *legato*. Schnabel was familiar with the techniques of half-pedal, quarter-pedal, etc., as described in Karl U. Schnabel's book *Modern Technique of the Pedal* (New York, 1950), but in my presence he never specifically taught these uses.

PROPORTIONS OF SOUND

These are dependent primarily on musical form and can therefore not be generally pre-determined. But, though few people know, there are laws that govern the ratio of loudness between several simultaneously-sounding notes.[1] Melodies are not usually found in the top part by chance, and inner parts frequently 'just stuffing', as Brahms used to say. Treble and bass, in that order, are more important than the rest. But a tenor melody, or a duplication in octaves of the melody or of harmony notes *can* exist, so that the rules which follow here—as Schnabel taught them—are only approximate.

(1) In a *four-part chord* in *close* position, the four notes are sounded as 'members of a family' with a slight preponderance of first the top,

[1] I doubt whether Schnabel was familiar with Tobias Matthay's *Musical Interpretation*, 1913–a diffuse book in which, however, some of these questions are dealt with.

then the bottom note above the rest. Example from the first movement of Schubert's Sonata in A minor, op. 42, bar 103 f:

Example 191

If the notes are far apart, the inner voices form a bridge between the outer ones and their sound becomes more important in proportion. In *pianissimo* and *fortissimo* passages special attention must be paid to the ratio between the highest voice and the others. In this way the pianist can avoid obscurities in a *pianissimo* and noisiness in a *fortissimo*. Pieces which require great volume for long periods, such as Schubert's *Wanderer* Fantasy or Schumann's *Symphonic Etudes*, absolutely demand this careful consideration. As a rule, even at full strength and greatest intensity of tone (as in the opening of the *Emperor* Concerto) the lower parts should be *mezzo forte*, the inner parts *mezzo piano*. What laymen call harshness of sound is usually produced by excess loudness of the *highest* parts. Schnabel once compared the two *sf* markings in bar 4 of Beethoven's *Pathétique* with each other: the first one is easily too harshly played, the second one, easily too loudly.

This distribution applies to strictly contrapuntal music as well. If two equally important parts are to be brought out with equal clarity they should not be played equally loudly. In a two-part setting the lower of the two parts must always be softer than the upper.

(2) In *octave duplications* the pianist must find out which is the principal (original) and which the duplicating part. Normally the lower octave duplicates the higher which must therefore be played louder and, where *legato* is called for, more *legato*. This is also true for left-hand octaves, despite the sound proportions of the natural harmonic scale in which the lower note is by far the louder one. Bass octaves on the piano must be handled like octaves written for 'cellos and double-basses. It means that the *legato* technique of right-hand octaves involves mainly the fourth and fifth fingers, whereas that wanted for the left hand concerns the thumb and thumb *legato* where

needed, most of all. The difference in loudness between the principal and the duplicating notes must be considerable. This is often neglected in ordinary scale passages, such as those occurring in the Finale of Beethoven's *Emperor* Concerto after the opening theme and in the final *stretto*. See also Beethoven's Polonaise, op. 89:

Example 192

The lower octave here is 'simply carried along'.

Exceptionally, the lower octave can lead – especially in slow expressive music, such as the middle episode from Beethoven's Sonata, op. 10 no. 3, second movement *Largo*.

Example 193

and Brahms's *Romanze*, op. 118 no. 5:

Example 194

One can sometimes discover this by looking at the beginning and the end of these passages to find out which of the two parts is connected with the directly preceding or directly following melody part. In the

Brahms example, moreover, the composer made his intentions clear by melody slurs, for the lower part only, in bars 2 and 3.

When there are three or four octaves at once, as for example in the development of Beethoven's *Emperor* Concerto, the top part is normally the original, and all others, duplications. When the top part is duplicated by its lower third as well as its lower octave, the *two* upper parts must be much louder than the lower octave, for they form a unit of sound, comparable to that of two people singing in thirds.

Example 195a

A good example: Brahms, Second Piano Concerto, first movement, bar 3; see Ex. 176 on p. 149. The rule remains the same even when there is another note played in addition, as in the near-final chord of Beethoven's Sonata in A flat, op. 110, five bars before the end, where the two top notes must be heard as a unit while the two lower notes played by the right hand are to sound much softer.

If the top line is duplicated by its lower octave and lower *sixth*, as happens so often in Brahms, a unit of sound is formed by the two *lower* voices. In relation to each other they must be softer than the top, but approximately equally loud.

Example 195b

(3) *Thirds and sixths*, without octave duplication, conform to the general rule that at the top the higher part, at the bottom, the lower part normally leads. See Beethoven's Bagatelle in G major, op.126 no. 1:

Example 196

(4) *Trills* are vibrations of the principal note. Since their problems are primarily technical, they will be discussed in the next chapter.

(5) *Root notes* of a chord—especially triads and seventh-chords—are important also when they occur in an inner part, particularly when they form a melodic connection as the common note of two successive chords. See Beethoven, op. 81a, *Les Adieux*, introduction, bars 12 ff.

Example 197

The B flat in the left hand is to be discreetly underlined, like a note played by a French horn. Other examples, Schubert, *Moment Musical*, op. 94 no. 6, Trio:

Example 198

Beethoven's Trio in B flat, op. 97, second part of variation theme; his C minor Variations, variation 23.

(6) When the melody is in a relatively high register, as compared to its accompanying chords, and when these chords are in close position—as throughout most of the slow movement of Mozart's Piano Concerto in C, K.467—the left hand must be very soft. Subconsciously we already supply normal chord progressions with our aural imagination. Unless the harmonies are quite unusual, a mere hint therefore will do. The situation is different only if the harmonies are unexpected, or if the left hand plays independent melodic parts rather than just chords or forms of Alberti basses, or also if the accompaniment is rhythmically individualized. The individual musical events in the lower parts can be brought out here, not only by articulation, but also by discreet dynamic emphases. If left hand

and right hand, in slow melodies, are very far apart (two octaves and more), the rule that inner notes must be much softer is suspended: it is sometimes good to lean on top notes in the left hand, and bottom notes in the right, simply as a means to create more of a link between registers.

(7) In the same order of ideas, if an arpeggio is played over an extended fraction of the keyboard—as happens in the Chromatic Fantasia of Bach, and also in the opening chord of the slow movement of Beethoven's Sonata in D minor, op. 31 no. 2:

Example 199

—in order to hear the chord as a unit Schnabel requested a *crescendo* towards the centre of the arpeggio and a *diminuendo* from there to the other end. This applies to arpeggios going in both directions. In other words, the proportions of loudness between the notes are the opposite from what they would be if the same notes were struck simultaneously. If the arpeggio occurs within the same register, however—as in Beethoven's Sonata, op. 109, bar 9—it is possible to disregard this rule and, in this example, make a steady *crescendo* from bottom to top. Thus it is always possible to observe dynamic markings in broken chords in a manner that is consistent with the principles announced here. In the Trio of the third movement of Beethoven's Sonata in E flat, op. 7, Schnabel held that the *fortissimo* markings, though literally marked only for the first note, have to be observed for the entire arpeggio—that is, for the first three notes in each bar marked thus.

Example 200

The rhythmic importance of Beethoven's marking is sufficiently secured by emphasizing the bass note in the left hand.

Broken thirds and octaves, etc. in the treble are treated like unbroken ones, which means that the *upper* third, octave, etc., although it is usually placed between the beats, must be played more loudly than the lower. See Mozart, Piano Concerto in C, K.467, Finale:

Example 201

Chopin, first *Impromptu*:

Example 202

The left hand, at the very beginning of Schumann's Sonata in G minor, plays a broken G minor chord. The note D′, although it forms the down-beat, must be softer than the B flat′ which is at the top.

Example 203

(8) In *figurations* made up of scales and chords, harmony notes must be heard as such. In Mozart's Piano Concerto in D minor, K.466, first movement, bar 98, the pianist should *not* play Ex. 204a, but Ex. 204b.

Example 204a, 204b

There is no need, however, for a special emphasis on the harmony notes since they all occur twice, whereas the passing notes come only once each.

PLAYING BOTH HANDS TOGETHER

Schnabel was violently opposed to the bad habit of the generations before him of playing the left hand before the right. He said jokingly that Beethoven must have devised the opening theme of the G major Sonata, op. 31 no. 1, as an étude to counteract this tendency. Normally he also avoided, within the notes played by the left hand, playing the lower notes before the upper ones. But there are instances when his hand, or that of a pupil, was too small to play all the notes at the same time as requested by the score. In these cases, which are frequent in the music of Schumann, Schnabel advised his pupils to play the bass together with the right hand on the beat, and to play the top note or notes of the left hand, very softly and unobtrusively, as soon as possible. See the Symphonic Etudes theme, bar 6:

Example 205a

In other words, no rolling of chords as in genuine arpeggios. The listener should be fooled into believing that all the notes were sounded simultaneously, whereas actually the note E in the left hand was played slightly later than the rest.

Example 205b

Through this technique Schnabel was able to discriminate between genuine arpeggios marked as such (either one hand after the other, or straight through both hands) and emergency arpeggios arising simply from limitations of the pianist's size of hand.

AVOIDANCE OF HARSHNESS AND OF GAPS IN SOUND

It has been mentioned before that harshness occurs when a note in the treble is played out of proportion with the rest of the music. When high notes alternate with low ones, within the same part, the low ones should be played clearly and fully in order to neutralize the change of register and level off the sound. This would apply to the melodic leaps at the end of the second movement of Beethoven's Sonata in E, op. 14 no. 1; to those of the theme of Mozart's Piano Concerto in A, K.488, slow movement; and also Beethoven's Sonata in C minor, op. 111, second movement, variation 4, bar 16. In all these movements, in order to bridge the melodic gaps, Schnabel declared that pedalling was necessary here: for the open dampers bridge any register change by increasing the overtone participation in the sound. In bar 153 of Brahms's Piano Concerto in D minor

Example 206

the third and fourth quavers of each unit must be stronger than the first and second, or else the latter will sound harsh.

Isolated *staccato* notes must be held long enough to evoke the necessary harmonic implications and to be heard in their intervallic connection with what precedes and what follows. The theme of the G minor Fugue of Book II of the *Well-Tempered Clavier* would be a good tune on which to practise this. Schnabel severely criticized the *staccato* playing of his pupils whenever they lost the musical connection, especially the melodic interval connection between successive notes, as soon as the *staccato* began. For them, he complained, 'music stops where *staccato* begins'. In Bach's works he cared only for the right articulation. He would sometimes take a prelude or fugue section from the *Well-Tempered Clavier* and play the same passage once *legato*, once *non-legato*, and once *staccato*, but so that the articulation remained equally clear in all three renderings. The point of this demonstration was to prove that quite often in Bach it is not vitally important to decide between these three types of touch, but that everything depends on the right declamation and coherence of the music.

When a melody note is repeated immediately, as on the down-beat following a last-second quick up-beat, the pianist should articulate the first note clearly enough to avoid ugly sounds. A good example occurs in Schubert's *Moment Musical* in A flat, op. 94 no. 2:

no. 2:

Example 207a   Example 207b

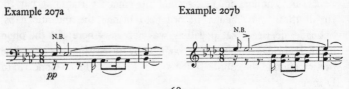

The accent sign in Ex. 207b does not change the music: it is simply made necessary by the difference in register.

Finally, the characteristic sound which Schnabel achieved in extremes of tempo and of dynamics, whether fast and loud, or fast and soft, etc., was largely an outcome of his mastery of the technique of *surprise*. He occasionally tried to teach this technique by saying, for instance, that a fast and brilliant passage will only be noticed as such if it comes surprisingly on top of slow and soft music without warning (as often in Chopin). Also his teaching of the very opening of piano pieces focused on the element of surprise. The surprise might consist of immediate full speed (as in Beethoven Sonatas such as the C major, op. 2 no. 3; B flat major, op. 22; G major, op. 79; D major for cello and piano, op. 102 no. 2) or in an unexpected degree of slowness (as in the Adagio movements of Beethoven's Sonata in E flat, op. 27 no. 1, or of his *Waldstein* Sonata, etc.). Whatever it was, Schnabel's extreme concentration on the sounds of the first bar—when the listener too is concentrating more than at any later time—always contained elements of surprise.

Throughout each piece, he did not play what the average music-lover expected to hear, but he impressed the music on the music-lover as much as on the professional musician by shedding a surprising new light on the composer's deepest meaning. This attitude implied the ruling out of most middle-of-the-road tempi and dynamics.

Obviously, from what has been stated earlier in this book, artificial surprises were never permissible. The element of surprise, as he heard it, was always anchored in the music itself, at least as a possibility. The best music, to Schnabel, was music in which surprises would or could occur; in which the tempo, for instance, could be taken much slower than anyone would have been able to expect. The unity of the performance was never in danger, because Schnabel not only thought of each piece as a whole, but also always kept a sound that was consistent in quality despite all these extremes. The reason I am speaking of the surprise element here, in a chapter on sound, is because its most noticeable effect was on the sonorities. But the same element also helps to explain some of the statements made in earlier chapters concerning Schnabel's way of phrasing, of grouping melodies metrically, of organizing *crescendi* through off-beat notes, etc. To surprise the listener as well as himself was one of Schnabel's most vital and valid impulses in his struggle for a complete exposition of articulation and structure.

CHAPTER TWELVE

Technique

From what was said in Chapter 2, it is clear that Schnabel conceived technique strictly as a means to a musical end. Whatever was necessary to achieve the desired musical result became part of technique, including special movements, fingerings, hand and finger positions, etc. In ordinary conservatory training certain ways of playing are sometimes considered 'illegal' tricks. In reality, there is no such thing. Musical masterpieces are distinguished from academic compositions by not adhering to all the rules all the time. It is impossible to anticipate and solve all the problems—including all the technical ones—arising in the interpretation of these great works in advance by following technical school rules. There *is* no fingering which a pianist must regard as taboo; no hand or finger position that must never be assumed; no method of touch that may not be used. There are only fingerings which are less usual; hand and finger positions which are seldom necessary; methods of touch only exceptionally called for in music. If they are unusual, the reason is that in a great majority of cases they do not serve the musical purpose. This is often so because they are in opposition to natural anatomy and the mechanical laws of motion. But exceptionally such ways and means may become not only effective but even necessary for the fulfilment of some musical goal, and the more exceptional the work to be played, the more frequent these instances are. This attitude of Schnabel's, among other things, accounts for some of the fingerings he proposed in his edition of the Beethoven Sonatas, especially the late ones.

Schnabel, according to his own statements, assumed that his pupils would have achieved a normal professional finger discipline before coming to study with him. He did not, therefore, have a 'system' of technique. He did communicate his personal approach to the solution of technical problems in general as well as of specific problems occurring in the pieces brought to him (the trills at the end of Beethoven's op. 111, the difficult jumps in the coda of the second movement of the Schumann Fantasy, etc.). He also gave general advice on the external details of playing, such as sitting low rather than high, using cold water on cold hands rather than warm, and so on.

Schnabel often spoke of music as being 'eloquent', and one can assume that his natural inclination to use speech inflections for the declamation of melodies and passages was further strengthened by the influence of his wife, Therese Schnabel, the famous *Lieder* singer whom he accompanied for many years. In keeping with this approach, he considered the physical activity of playing as a gesture akin to rhetoric. As I mentioned earlier, he spoke of playing as going 'forward and out' rather than down (which inevitably results from throwing fingers, hands or arms). In a conversation I had with him in 1951 he contrasted his physical approach with that of certain well-known virtuosi. Instead of sitting forward, holding the fingers on top of the keys, he preferred to sit relatively far away from the keyboard so that the hand would reach it by a forward stretch of the arms, approaching it from below. The usual finger stroke was thus eliminated.[1] The key went down as a result of a slight raising of the whole arm while the fingertip was already touching the surface of the key. This, he assured me, gave him much greater immediate control and enabled him to play with such relaxation that he could engage spontaneously in free rhythms of declamation. He claimed that the opposite way rendered the pianist capable of playing only exactly as he had practised.

Having acquired a fluent finger technique at an early age, he did not fully realize that a less than technically perfect pupil could easily be confused by this approach. Many, at least at first, pushed stiff arms forward, raising wrists in the process and thus making it

---

[1] Nevertheless, he occasionally spoke of the 'need for steel fingers' in special places, as in the development of Beethoven's Fourth Piano Concerto, first movement, bars 216–229 (C-sharp minor).

impossible to achieve any finger control at all. He emphasized that complete physical relaxation, including neck and shoulders,[1] was the necessary preliminary condition under which his technique would work. He advised the student to gain this relaxation by a greater intensity of detailed listening. He would practise, for instance, full chords so that he could hear exactly each single note in its proportion to the others. In this way he was able to play chords with no stiffening of the muscles and 'with shoulder participation' (Breithaupt) as a natural result.

It was consistent with his theory that he did not speak of weight falling on the keys, but of weight being brought forward. He once illustrated this by placing his flat hands on his knees and moving the elbows forward so that the fingers would bend at the knuckles and support the arm weight. Weight playing of this kind, he said, made it possible 'to walk freely on firm ground'. In general though, physical demonstrations of this kind were not to his liking because, as a matter of principle, he was against isolating the elements which come together in the act of music-making. For this reason he did not approve of the rhythmic clapping and tapping exercises of the Dalcroze school and considered them artificial isolations of one element. 'I myself cannot do these exercises,' he said, 'although I can play complicated polymetric figurations. I always need to hear the pitch.' He firmly believed that the complete awareness of the musical goal, intensely clear in every detail, provides every performer with the necessary means to get there.

His method of practising was experiment rather than drill. He was against slow practising of fast passages as a general habit, against the practising of each hand alone as such, and against the old device of practising even semiquavers as dotted rhythms of one kind or another. He considered études a waste of time: 'they are too easy,' he said, 'because the same difficulty comes again and again, while in a Mozart concerto you meet various kinds of technical difficulties in one single bar, and usually only get one chance to work them out.' The occasion for this remark was the following passage (Mozart, Concerto in C, K.467, bar 169):

[1] See Chapter 2, p. 24

Example 208

Instead he recommended inventing melodic sequences of any pattern posing technical problems; i.e. composing one's own studies whenever these were needed.

His practice time was devoted to working out the exact articulation of a piece. He worked over each phrase hundreds of times to find the fingering, the hand position, the finger and arm movements that would secure the perfect inflection of melody, rhythm and harmony which he heard inwardly.

To his pupils he defined practising as 'passing the day at the piano with patience and serenity', and this, as far as I know, is what he did himself. He was entirely honest when he stated that his occasional nervousness was mainly due to the fact that music makes higher demands on the performer than he is capable of at a given moment, or perhaps, at any time.

Of the various ways of articulating it was mainly the melodic articulation, the eloquent declamation, which became important for his technical approach and thus the focal point of his practising. In all figurations, especially in Mozart concertos, he mentally grouped notes according to their upward or downward direction, proceeding from note to note, yet keeping the general melodic line in mind.

Example 209a

The above example from the first movement of Mozart's Concerto in G, K.453, bar 153, was analysed for practice purposes as follows:

Example 209b

In this way the general melodic line is clarified.

Example 209c

See also the opening of the solo part, bar 74.

Obviously this principle is valid for the articulation of slow passages (as in the middle sections of the slow movements of the Mozart Sonatas in G major, K.283 and D major, K.576) as well as of fast ones. Schnabel, who practised such slow passages as meticulously as so-called 'virtuoso' ones, had little patience with pupils who only worked over the 'difficult' spots. He devoted much time to slow figurations, including Alberti basses.[1]

We have seen how Schnabel's concern for changes of melodic direction within the same passage led him to focus some attention on the technical problem arising from the use of the fourth finger following the fifth in scale passages. In his own playing of chromatic and diatonic scales (of the kind to be found, for instance, in Beethoven's Fourth Piano Concerto) they came off with *glissando*-like continuity *and* adagio-like melodic quality. He hated listening to 'scales with moth-holes'. The same musical approach guided his playing of the scale passages in Weber's *Invitation to the Dance*, the Schubert Impromptus in E flat, op. 90 no. 2 and B flat (last variation), op. 142 no. 3, and the left-hand run at the beginning of the last movement of Beethoven's Sonata in G, op. 14 no. 2. In all these passages, as in the broken thirds and octaves so frequently found in Mozart concertos, Schnabel would think in terms of the entire phrase and not of the single note, and in performance he would listen to each note not by itself but as part of a larger unit. In the same way he conceived and executed arpeggios as broken chords, as for example at the opening of the Scherzo of Brahms's Sonata in F minor. He was convinced that this could not be done with the ordinary percussive finger stroke from above, but only with his kind

[1] See p. 105.

of forward playing coming from below in which he could conduct the lateral motions with the help of his relaxed and active elbow. Thinking in terms of large units made the playing, no matter how fast, *feel* slow to him, and he always recommended for such passages to 'play slow and sound fast', a surprisingly effective psychological device.

Polyphonic playing, to Schnabel, was entirely the product of polyphonic hearing. He took the necessary finger independence for granted[1] and advised his pupils to practise polyphony by first studying each voice melodically, so that it would be recognizable no matter where it might be situated, simply by lucid articulation. After this the interpreter had to establish a 'hierarchy' between the several simultaneous melodies. Schnabel used to exclaim: 'If you cannot think in several voices at the same time, give up the piano and learn the clarinet', but he also admitted that this faculty could be trained. He recommended, for instance, playing three parts of a four-part fugue while singing the fourth part, repeating this process with all four parts in turn, and then, while playing all four together, listening specifically to each part in turn. Here as always he was against practising separate hands, since the inner parts are normally distributed between the hands.[2] Their articulation is one of the main goals to be secured in polyphonic playing. He did advise listening to string quartets while following the score, paying particular attention, horizontally, to the 2nd violin and viola. To him this was part of *technical* practising.

His control in polyphonic playing enabled him to clarify the many chamber-music–like passages in Schubert, as at the end of the exposition of the first movement of his Sonata in B, or in the Minuet of the same work, bar 19:

[1] He knew, however, that the different strength of individual fingers could present problems and he said half-jokingly that one should play polyphonic music with crossed hands so that the strongest fingers would serve the outer parts.

[2] In *linear* music, when it was distributed between the two hands, he liked to play (or, at least, practise) everything with one hand; for example at the beginning of variation 2 of Beethoven's Sonata, op. 109, Finale.

Example 210a

Here he wanted to be sure that the performer heard the 'viola' melody clearly, if delicately, below the right-hand parts.

Example 210b

As a technical exercise, he suggested playing all five fingers together in five-finger position and in the same hand combine any *legato* melody with these notes; for instance C-D-E-F-G-E-F-D-C, or:

Example 211

Schnabel's *trills* had a special quality and he was often asked to explain how he played them. He would occasionally give an answer in terms of physical movement, such as keeping the arm high, the fingers loose and the wrist and elbow sufficiently fixed to permit a shake from the upper arm; or using fingers other than neighbouring ones wherever possible. This was what he also used for repeated octaves (as in Schubert's *Erlkönig*) or *tremolos*, only the spirit was different. Essentially, Schnabel heard trills as what they are in singing, namely the vibration of a single note. With very few exceptions this referred to the lower tone of the trill, and Schnabel listened to its rapid repeats rather than to both trill notes equally. The result was that the two notes were even in their timing but uneven in strength, the auxiliary note being softer than the principal note.[1] The trill was always played as rapidly as possible so that it would be just a vibration, avoiding an accent on the very first beginning, so as to get the motion fully going at once. Played this way, the trill could have an almost 'transcendental power' when it occurred at a decisive place in the music, as at the end of Beethoven's Sonata, op. 111, or at the end of the slow movement of Brahms's First Piano Concerto in D minor.

To Schnabel, all other considerations came first in time; the job of reducing wrong notes last. Nevertheless he was quite careful in working out technical details. As his published editions of classical works show, he spent considerable effort in finding appropriate fingerings. He often spoke of 'handings' rather than fingerings because he thought primarily in terms of hand positions. The fingerings he worked out served not only the music but technical security also by permitting the hand to stay in a natural position. To this end he would frequently play neighbouring notes with non-adjacent fingers, especially with 3 and 5, omitting the fourth finger. This permitted him to use the fifth finger with its full length, that is, stretched as far forward over the keys as possible.[2] He ridiculed the traditional training (to which he himself had been subjected as a child) in which the hand had to remain so motionless that a coin placed on it would not fall. On the contrary he advocated letting the hand move in all three dimensions and in all possible directions around the keyboard, wherever it would feel most natural, using naturally curved as well as naturally stretched fingers, depending on the technical and musical demands of the moment. In this manner he was able to adjust instantly to changes in dynamics without a visible change in the position or movement of the hands. In a sudden *fortissimo* this was sometimes amazing to watch, and it heightened the surprise effect

[1] It is obvious that this trill technique must be slightly different for the two hands, as the principal note is played with the inner finger in the right hand and the outer finger in the left. The difference in Schnabel's technique came about exclusively through appropriate weight distribution.

[2] In his interview with James F. Cooke (see Chapter 2, p. 24) Schnabel described how he would bend the wrist in and out to compensate for the shortness of thumb and fifth finger. I never heard him teach this.

without interrupting the continuous, even quality of sound, for instance in the middle section of Brahms's Intermezzo in E flat minor, op. 118 no. 6. His freedom of movement was secured by constant closeness to the keyboard. The keys seemed to emit a magnetic attraction for his fingertips, no matter in which way the hand was being held. To the onlooker it seemed that the keys were completely covered and protected by his hands.

The fact that wrong notes could not be avoided in his concerts and even his recordings[1] is no reflection on his technique, for it is due entirely to his total concentration on the music at the moment of performance. He did not ever permit himself to sacrifice some detail of articulation or the intensity of immediate expression to caution and security. He often made fun of the "emergency *maëstoso*" (as at the end of Brahms's Capriccio, op. 116 no. 1) with which some pianists would mask their concern for the right notes at the expense of musical drive.

[1] They all precede the use of spliceable tape.

APPENDIX

Schnabel's Lessons

Only in rare cases were Schnabel's lessons private. Usually, some or most of his pupils would be present during lessons, but he sincerely ignored them altogether, and never addressed his remarks to anybody but the pupil being taught at the time. There was no fixed time for the length of a lesson. The minimum duration was one-and-a-half hours, but I have seen him give lessons of close on three hours. In his later years, when he lived in New York and taught in a very small room—using a Steinway upright himself, while his pupils would play on his Steinway grand—he could not have more than two or three others listening, and he normally gave two-hour lessons.

Each lesson was entirely filled with the specific piece which the pupil brought to him. There were no exercises, scales, studies, etc. checked or discussed. The piece was selected by the pupil. With very few exceptions Schnabel did not assign pieces to his pupils. At the beginning of the lesson, the pupil would play the whole piece—or the whole movement if the work was in several movements—without interruptions, and without the music.[1] Schnabel would take the score belonging to the pupil, and he would sometimes pencil something in or circle a wrongly-remembered chord while the performance was in progress. At the end, after a short silence, the verdict would come in certain types of verbal reactions: 'very good' (this meant a lot!); 'well . . .' (basic concept wrong or questionable); or 'bravo' (this was capital punishment! It meant: too much attention to brilliant technique, and neglect of the music). After this, Schnabel usually described in general what he thought the main problem of the performer was on that day: not enough control; too passive; not enough colour or intensity; etc., etc. From then on, his attention was exclusively focused on the piece itself and its demands, and no longer on the student's personal development.

Section after section was most minutely taken apart. Schnabel

[1] Concertos he accompanied himself.

would explain what, to him, was important in the opening phrase and sit down and play that phrase once or twice, then turn round to the other piano and say: 'try'. Then he would criticize every detail of the imitation which the pupil attempted, especially refinements of accentuation, proportion of parts, dynamic plan, polyphonic clarity (in so-called 'homophonic' music as well: each voice, in a simple accompanying chord, had to come from the preceding and had to go on to the following chord). Like a conductor in an orchestral rehearsal, Schnabel would let the pupil repeat a phrase (usually without playing it again himself) until it sounded right to his ear, even if it took twenty repetitions. He would sing it, conduct it, invent words to an instrumental melody in order to get the right declamation, walk to it, make dance steps, explain poetically and philosophically why this phrase had to sound the way he wanted it; etc. Only very rarely would he look at the pupil's hands and attempt to get the right declamation and expression through specific technical means, but occasional general hints, as described previously in this book, about flexible elbows, 'forward' playing, etc., were forthcoming in almost every lesson.

And so it would go on, phrase by phrase, until the end of the movement. The rate of progress was so slow that in one lesson not more than one or one-and-a-half movements of normal length could be dealt with. Schnabel did not attempt to link the various sections together in another complete performance at the end; this was left to the pupil. In general, during his later years, he heard each piece but once. With mature players, he was quite tolerant of deviating conceptions, and often suggested alternative solutions to problems of phrasing and dynamics. Even then, there was little discussion, and we were of course interested in how *he* did it. Schnabel did not like his pupils—both those who were playing and those who were attending the lesson as listeners—to take notes or mark their scores according to his dicta. 'What I say here,' he said, 'ought to be remembered not as words, but *as music*.' He never attempted to drill or browbeat his pupils, once they had understood what he wanted and could tentatively imitate it. 'The teacher can only open the door; it is for the pupil to pass through it.'[1]

[1] Artur Schnabel, *My Life and Music*, p. 130.

Conclusion

Schnabel's approach to articulation, to score-reading, to interpretation in its various aspects, and to the problems of sonority and technique was individual and complex. In the preceding pages I have tried to report faithfully whatever I was able to gather at the time and to remember. Any attempt to criticize Schnabel's views, as expressed in his teaching, would have resulted in distortions and confusions. If my report is clear, it will be easy for anyone to accept, reject, or amend any part of it, or to build a more complete aesthetic system on this or that aspect of Schnabel's views.

His individuality and complexity, however, should not obscure the fact that Schnabel, as an artistic personality, was homogeneous and harmonious. What he taught – pianistically as well as musically – came naturally to him, without struggle and effort. His extravagant metrical solutions, for instance, were an outcome of his playful imagination, and the various 'rules' governing sonorities resulted directly from his instinct for sensuous beauty of sound. A composer himself, he combined with this due respect for the intentions of the great masters and an insatiable curiosity, trying to revive the mystery of their creations in performance, entering deeper and deeper into their spirit with each attempt at 'identification'. It is with this in mind that the reader of this book will have to guard himself against translating it into external rules and easy solutions. What this book, at best, may accomplish is to make young musicians sensitive to certain ways of inward listening. They may perhaps also be helped to enjoy the activity of playing more than before as they begin to use a natural technique, that is, a technique in which the expression is served naturally. And scholars may find original solutions to some old problems of rhythm, melody, harmony, etc., in Schnabel's unstudied and spontaneous presentation of all the musical elements.

Index

(Page numbers containing examples are printed in italics. Movements are listed in roman numerals: 'op. 31, 2, II' = opus 31, number 2, second movement.)